W. Michael Hoffman is Director of the Center for Business Ethics and Chair of the Philosophy Department at Bentley College. He received his Ph.D. in philosophy from the University of Massachusetts at Amherst. Hoffman has published numerous articles in various professional journals and has lectured on metaphysics, philosophy of religion, business ethics, philosophical ecology, and the history of ideas. In addition, he is the author of *Kant's Theory of Freedom: A Metaphysical Inquiry.* Hoffman has received grants from the National Endowment for the Humanities, the Matchette Foundation, and the Council for Philosophical Studies.

Jennifer Mills Moore is Research Associate at the Center for Business Ethics and Adjunct Instructor of Philosophy at Bentley College. She did her undergraduate work at Bowdoin College and is currently completing doctoral work in philosophy and religious studies at Harvard University.

Hoffman and Moore are coauthors of a special edition of the *Journal of Business Ethics* which is devoted to presentations given at the Center's first three National Conferences on Business Ethics. They are coauthors of the article "What is Business Ethics? A Reply to Peter Drucker." In addition, they are coauthoring an anthology on business ethics, to be published by McGraw-Hill.

ETHICS AND THE MANAGEMENT OF COMPUTER TECHNOLOGY

Aerial view of Bentley College, Cedar Hill, Waltham, Massachusetts.

Ethics and the Management of Computer Technology

Proceedings of the
Fourth National Conference
on Business Ethics

Sponsored by
The Center for Business Ethics
Bentley College

Edited by
W. Michael Hoffman
Jennifer Mills Moore
Bentley College

 Oelgeschlager, Gunn & Hain, Publishers, Inc.
Cambridge, Massachusetts

International Standard Book Number: 0-89946-144-1

Library of Congress Catalog Card Number: 82-3562

Printed in West Germany

Library of Congress Cataloging in Publication Data

National Conference on Business Ethics (4th:
  1981: Bentley College)
  Ethics and the management of computer
technology.

  Includes bibliographical references.
  1. Electronic data processing—Moral and
ethical aspects—Congresses. 2. Business ethics
Jennifer Mills. I. Hoffman, W. Michael. II. Moore,
Business Ethics. IV. Title.
QA76.9.M65N37 1981   174'.4   82-3562
ISBN 0-89946-144-1   AACR2

Contents

v

Preface

W. Michael Hoffman*

The Center for Business Ethics at Bentley College was founded in 1976 for the primary purpose of providing a non-partisan forum for the exchange of ideas on business ethics in an industrial society, particularly as these ideas relate to the activities of corporations, labor, government, special interest groups, and the professions. The Center thus far has sponsored four National Conferences on Business Ethics in which some of our nation's most influential leaders and thinkers have participated and which literally hundreds of representatives from various constituencies all over the country have attended. It is hoped that these conferences have fostered and will continue to foster greater awareness and understanding of moral issues within our business world from diverse perspectives.

The Center has published the proceedings of these conferences in book form. *The Proceedings of the First National Conference on Business Ethics: Business Values and Social Justice—Compatibility or Contradiction?* was published in 1977 by the Center. *The Proceedings of the Second National Conference on Business Ethics: Power and Responsibility in the American Business System* was published in 1979 by the University Press of America, Inc., in Washington, D.C. *The Work Ethic in Business: Proceedings of the Third National Conference on Business Ethics* was published in 1981 by Oelgeschlager, Gunn & Hain, Inc., the publishers of this volume. These works have been purchased by hundreds of organizations and individuals for research in the field of business ethics and are being used in many business ethics courses throughout the country.

*Director, The Center for Business Ethics; Professor and Chair, Department of Philosophy, Bentley College

In addition to the conferences and *Proceedings,* the Center publishes *Business Ethics Reports* which describe the highlights of the conferences, various bibliographies on business ethics, and collections of syllabi of business ethics courses. It also videotapes the proceedings of the conferences and makes these tapes available for sale or rental, and conducts surveys relating to business ethics. Furthermore, the Center serves as a general clearinghouse for ideas and information concerning the field of business ethics studies and moral issues connected to business activities. We believe that as a result of this work the Center has helped to create a climate of greater understanding and trust among various constituencies and has furthered its ultimate aim of establishing a better ethical framework within which to conduct business in general. It is the conviction of the Center that without the input of ideas from all important facets of our business world, the ethical dilemmas which so seriously threaten the very existence and meaningfulness of our lives will never be approached successfully.

The Fourth National Conference on Business Ethics and other activities of the Center for Business Ethics at Bentley College were made possible in part from grants from the following: Arvin Industries; Robert W. Brown, M.D.; The Council for Philosophical Studies (sponsored by the National Endowment for the Humanities); Exxon Education Foundation; The General Mills Foundation; General Motors Corporation; Midland-Ross, Inc.; The Motorola Foundation; The Raytheon Charitable Foundation; Rexnord, Inc.; Richardson-Merrill, Inc.; The Rockefeller Foundation; Semline, Inc.; Stop and Shop Manufacturing Companies; and F. W. Woolworth Company. On behalf of the Center, I wish to thank all of these contributors and all the participants of the Fourth National Conference for sharing with us their support and ideas.
I am also pleased to take this opportunity to formally express our appreciation to Jeremiah J. O'Connell, Dean of Bentley's Graduate School, who served as Conference Chairman. The success of this Fourth National Conference was largely due to his vision and dedication to ethical goals for managers of computer technology.
Finally, a special thanks must go to Ann Forestell and Susan Zimmerman of the Center for Business Ethics for their help toward the preparation and organization of this volume.

Introduction

*Jennifer Mills Moore**

The papers collected in this volume represent the deliberations and discussions which took place at Bentley College's Fourth
National Conference on Business Ethics, on the ethical management of computer technology. The traditional relationship between
business and technology makes the topic an appropriate one for a
conference on business ethics; the relationship has been one of
mutual nourishment and support. Business values—such as those
of productivity, efficiency, growth—have guided the development
and use of new technologies, mediating their impact on society at
large. Technologies in turn have shaped the manner and context in
which business is conducted. The importance of such interrelation-
ships is magnified in the case of revolutionary technological developments, like that of the computer. As business continues to make
significant financial, structural, and managerial commitments to
computer technology, an examination of its ethical implications
becomes increasingly urgent.

A second reason for the importance of ethical reflection on computer technology can be found in the widespread conviction that
technology, with business, inhabits an amoral sphere in which
ethical values, standards, and judgments are inappropriate or irrelevant. The source of this conviction lies in a comprehensive ideological framework—a framework to which business ethics and kindred disciplines pose a serious challenge.

Our society has been weaned on relativism, the denial of abso-
lutes; pragmatism, the belief that something is right if it works;
positivism, the identification of knowledge with what is verifiable
by observation or experience; and behaviorism, the conviction that
human action is completely predictable. The result of this cluster of
ideas has been the reduction of what is considered true and meaningful to the material, the quantitative, the empirically verifiable.

*Research Associate, Center for Business Ethics; Adjunct Instructor of Philos-
ophy, Bentley College

In such a philosophical context, facts and values are cut off from each other; values are severed from the rational and the meaningful and exiled to the sphere of the subjective emotions. And if ethical values truly are entities beyond the reach of reason's grasp, they can have no place in business or technological decison-making. It is not surprising, therefore, that many professionals have come to see themselves as operating in a "value-free" realm, one in which ethical criteria of evaluation simply do not apply. Some thinkers have argued explicitly that business is just such a morally neutral activity, with its own inevitably amoral rules and goals.[1] Surely it is tempting to conclude the same of technology—particularly, perhaps, of computer technology, which is governed by a language and a logic in which ethical values literally "do not compute."

Like Bentley's three previous business ethics conferences, the Fourth National Conference on Business Ethics challenges the possibility of meaningful but value-free human activity. It represents the conviction that technological choices like those made in the management of computer technology are not morally neutral, but value-laden. The mere appearance of computers on the technological scene reflects the goals and priorities held by our society. And computers carry with them consequences the evaluation of which requires more than a simple cost-benefit analysis. It is the word "simple" which misleads here, since the question of what is to count as a "cost" and what as a "benefit"—an ethical question—must be answered before such an analysis can be made. New technologies thus confront us with a demand for the reexamination of what it is we really value, and bring a freshness of vision to the examination process. Because it both reflects and shapes our values, then, computer technology invites—indeed, compels—ethical deliberation.

These *Proceedings* contain a diversity of positions on a broad spectrum of ethical issues in the management of computer technology. Some participants are optimistic about a future enhanced by the capabilities of computers; others are more circumspect. They have in common the rejection of an amoral computer technology and a commitment to the ethical perspective. In his introduction to the conference, Bentley President Gregory H. Adamian affirms that the College shares this commitment, a commitment which has been reflected in the activities of Bentley's Center for Business Ethics since its inception. Each presentation or panel at the conference was followed by a period of open discussion, the texts of which have been included in these *Proceedings*. In editing this volume, we have attempted to preserve the spontaneity of both

presentations and discussions—a spontaneity we feel is characteristic of the free exchange of ideas.

Joseph Coates, president of the consulting firm J. F. Coates, Inc.,
opened the conference, emphasizing the vast scope of the changes
that could be effected by the widespread use of computer technology.
Because of this scope, and because the computer could act either as
a powerful promoter or as a serious threat to human autonomy,
Coates urges careful, foresighted, normative reflection on the use
of computer technology. Not only have we not yet begun to engage
in such reflection in an effective way, he believes; in fact, confron-
tation with computer technology reveals our entire tradition of
ethical thought as bankrupt. We continue to rely on the personal-
istic ethics of the Judeo-Christian tradition, which can no longer
give us guidance in a society dominated by organizations. We place
too much trust in the "invisible hand" of the market system to promote the welfare of society at large. Coates points to the ethical
failure of the market system and seems to call for a communitarian
ethics which would emphasize systemic values and the place of the
individual in the organization.

Using some of the issues raised by Coates as a springboard, James
Emery of the Wharton School and Abbe Mowshowitz of the Croton
Research Group examine the source of potential clashes between
computer technology and human values. A majority of the threats
to human values by computer technology, Emery believes, stem
not from the technology itself at all, but from failures in design and
implementation. He invokes the fundamental professional responsibility of computer technologists to build excellent systems—systems, perhaps, which preserve and reflect our values without dis-
tortion. Good systems can of course be used for evil purposes, Emery
admits. But his greater fear is of the risks inherent in reliance on
poorly designed systems.

Mowshowitz takes issue with Emery's implication that computer
technology is a neutral tool, the ethical implications of which depend solely upon how it is used. Because of its particular capabilities, Mowshowitz argues, and because of the social and historical
situation in which it is introduced, every technology carries with
it "biases" which affect our lives in complex and far-reaching ways.
Computer technology, like all technologies, demands adaptations
on the part of society in return for the benefits it promises. Mowshowitz focuses primarily on the contribution of the computer to
the increasing centralization and remoteness of social control. He
believes that computer technology fosters fragmentation, reductionism, the separation of control from performance, and—echoing

a theme from Coates's presentation—the potential atrophy of the capacity for autonomous decision-making itself.

In his "Ethical Dilemmas in Computer Technology," Donn Parker of Stanford Research Institute International shifts the focus of discussion away from the impact of the computer on society at large and toward ethical issues confronted by the computer professional. Computer technology is changing the nature of white-collar crime, Parker suggests. His presentation of instances of "data diddling," "Trojan horses" and "logic bombs" highlights both our dependence on and our lack of control over computer technology—a lack of control which makes us vulnerable to attacks from a highly skilled, criminal elite.

Through research conducted using a scenario technique, Parker has discovered a profound disagreement and confusion among computer professionals over ethical issues, and in some cases failure to identify ethical issues at all. The failure of the educational process to impart ethical values to students for the use of computers is one source of confusion. Another is the fostering of an amoral or "game-playing" mentality by professors who frankly encourage students to undermine university computer systems as a learning exercise. Parker calls for an assumption of responsibility on the part of educators and emphasizes the need for a consensus on standards of behavior for computer professionals.

Taking up Parker's challenge to educators, Deborah Johnson of Rensselaer Polytechnic Institute and Jeffrey Meldman of the Massachusetts Institute of Technology's Sloan School of Management describe their own work in educating toward ethical responsibility in the use of computers. Like Parker, Johnson sees a simple failure to recognize some issues as ethical at all to be one of the major stumbling blocks in teaching ethics to computing students. In addition, she believes, her students have been nurtured in a quantitative, technological intellectual environment. They are ill equipped to deal with ethical issues and are inclined to take such issues less than seriously because they are not susceptible to familiar intellectual tools. In addition, Johnson reports, the structure and politics of many educational institutions can discourage courses in the ethical management of computer technology. Such a course is not, strictly, a "computing" course, and may not be perceived as essential to the career of a computer professional. Despite these difficulties, both Johnson and Meldman claim a modest success at instilling students with an awareness of ethical issues and at providing a framework for ethical decision-making.

Meldman suggests that ethical behavior be presented pragmatically to students as a prerequisite for an overall "good system."

There are ethical reasons for building good systems, he concurs with James Emery; conversely, acting responsibly can be viewed as a pragmatic imperative. In closing, Meldman urges business organizations to share responsibility for ethical education with the academic world by providing a climate in which responsible decision-making is supported and encouraged.

The third panel of the conference turns attention toward strategies for the ethical management of computer technology in corporate and public institutions. Speakers Elizabeth Byrne Adams, president of the consulting firm Management/Technology Interface, Inc., and W. Forest Horton, former director of the Federal Paperwork Commission, urge organizations to take positive steps toward the recognition and management of information as a valuable resource. Adams stresses the inefficiency and lack of organization which characterizes the use of information assets in most institutions today. The solution, she believes, is Information Resource Management, a way of "organizing information flows and information-handling technologies to accomplish organizational objectives" that maximizes control, efficiency, and accountability with respect to information resources. Both Adams and Horton call for the appointment of an "information resource manager" who will oversee the management of information throughout the organization. Such a manager would hold a position of tremendous power, Horton points out. In particular, information resource managers placed in governmental positions might be tempted to abuse that power by withholding information from the public, invading privacy, or even seizing more power. Steps must be taken to minimize such risks, Horton concludes, since the information resource manager is virtually a necessity in the modern organization.

Arthur Miller of Harvard Law School elaborates on an issue raised only briefly by Horton—that of the potential of computer technology for the violation of individual privacy rights. The tremendous increase in privacy-related legislation, he suggests, illustrates the seriousness of public concern over the threats posed to privacy by the computer. Miller cites four of the public's legitimate privacy-oriented fears with respect to computer technology: The introduction of the computer makes practicable a massive amount of data collection and storage. People fear the sheer amount of the information collected about them and feel that they have no control over it or its use. Data collection capabilities in turn make it possible to make decisions (such as the admission of candidates to universities) by file, by data, and by number, which were previously made in other ways. It is feared that computerized decision-making leads to reductionism, depersonalization, and the erosion of autonomy as human beings are cut off from the immediacy of their choices. A third area of concern is that of the use of data out of context. Although computers facilitate the mobility of data, Miller explains, a new context often makes the original data difficult to interpret or even irrelevant. Failure to recognize this fact can lead to the serious misuse of information. Perhaps the greatest fear of all, however, is that associated with governmental data collection. Information is power, Miller states; as the government obtains more information about its citizens, its power and its potential for controlling the behavior of the public increases. In closing, Miller offers some ethical principles for the use of computer technology which could help to reduce the threat of computers to privacy.

In the final panel of the conference, James Brian Quinn of Dartmouth's Tuck School and Sidney Schoeffler of The Strategic Planning Institute return to the broader issues of the impact of the computer on society and examine the relationship of computer technology to strategic planning.

Quinn details some of the potential benefits of computers on both the domestic and international scenes. Computer technology can increase the number of jobs, he suggests, and greatly improve the quality of working life. It can enhance the power of the individual in society by making possible a true referendum democracy. It can foster a more aware, more informed, and thus more autonomous public. At the international level, computer technology can speed the progress of developing countries, break down parochial nationalism, and aid in the birth of a genuine worldwide community. Harking back to a point made by Coates, Quinn warns against basing decisions in the management of computer technology on short-term, economic expediency. He calls for the replacement of purely economic indicators with new, "values-produced-per-person" social indicators in making strategic choices for social welfare.

The widespread use of computer technology not only demands strategic choice, Schoeffler indicates; it can itself make significant contributions in the development of personal, business, or social stragegy. Schoeffler disagrees with Arthur Miller about the dangers of massive data collection and computerized decision-making. On the contrary, he contends, an extensive data-base is a prerequisite to truly informed, rational, and scientific choice. His own institute has successfully used computer technology in long-term strategic planning for businesses. Schoeffler suggests that the same techniques adopted by individuals could enable them to live more satisfying and productive lives.

In his "Fast Machines and Slow Minds," Clarence Walton of the

American College sums up the themes of the conference by citing six crucial areas of concern for the ethical management of computer technology: the impact of computer technology on the job market and its meaning for the quality of working life; the role of big business and the market system in directing the uses to which computer technology is put; the potential of computer technology for the violation of individual freedom and privacy; the possibility of the increasing powerlessness of individuals in the face of a computer technology controlled by organizations and/or information resource managers; the danger of the submergence of personal goals or irrelevance of the Judeo-Christian ethical tradition as a guide in choices concerning the management of computer technology. Part of the value of new technological developments, Walton suggests, lies in the fact that they force us to examine issues like these—as well as to rethink such fundamental questions as the nature of persons, the dimensions of human rights, the meaning and character of a moral community. He ends on a note of exhortation, inviting the members of the conference to address themselves to the questions he has outlined and to participate in the construction of a new, ethically rooted civilization.

Perhaps the single most important theme which emerges from the presentations and discussions of the Fourth National Conference on Business Ethics is that of human autonomy—its assumption or abdication. The frequency with which words like "freedom," "power," "knowledge," "control," "responsibility"—all of which are aspects of autonomy—appear in these discussions is striking. On the one hand, it is suggested that computer technology can increase our autonomy by giving us more freedom in work and leisure, by placing vast amounts of information at our disposal, by improving communications and enhancing participative democracy, and by bringing us new forms of control over the environment in which we live. At the same time, it is felt that computer technology can contribute to the domination of individuals by organizations, to the separation of control from task performance, to the concentration of power in the hands of a new, high-technology elite, and to increased governmental authority over the lives of individuals.

The fact that our choices can determine which of these sets of effects of computer technology will prevail highlights the importance of a more fundamental, more subtle threat to autonomy suggested by some of the conference speakers. Computer technology requires significant adaptations by those who wish to exploit its advantages; some fundamental values may be lost in the adaptation process. As decision-making becomes increasingly computer-dominated, it becomes increasingly automated, depersonalized, and quantitative. It is possible that the very capacity to reflect on value-related issues may be undermined. The difficulty that technologically oriented students have in identifying ethical issues ought perhaps to be viewed as a warning of this trend. Writes Professor of Computer Science Joseph Weizenbaum,

> ...we have permitted technological metaphors...and technique itself to so thoroughly pervade our thought processes that we have finally abdicated to technology the very duty to...formulate important questions for us—questions whose very forms severely diminish the number of degrees of freedom in our range of decision-making. Whoever dictates the questions in large part determines the answers.[2]

Weizenbaum urges us to assume the responsibility for formulating questions about ourselves, our goals and values, and the use of our technology. The Fourth National Conference on Business Ethics represents at least a significant beginning of this important task.

NOTES

1. See, for example, John Ladd, "Is 'Corporate Responsibility' a Coherent Notion?" *Proceedings of the Second National Conference on Business Ethics,* ed. W. Michael Hoffman (Waltham, Mass.: Bentley College, 1977).
2. Joseph Weizenbaum, "On the Impact of the Computer on Society," *Social Effects of Computer Use and Misuse,* ed. J. Mack Adams and Douglas H. Haden (New York: John Wiley and Sons, 1976), pp. 280, 281.

Introduction to the Conference

Gregory H. Adamian[*]

Welcome to Bentley College and to the Fourth National Conference on Business Ethics. As an institution founded for, and still largely committed to, professional studies in business, Bentley College could choose to graduate the finest technocrats in accounting, management, and computer information systems. We have, however, chosen to walk the steeper, less well charted path of graduating the liberally educated professional. We stand astride C. P. Snow's two cultures, more convinced of the necessity to bridge the worlds of values and business than possessed of any infallible formula to design and engineer this educational synthesis.

We dare not give exclusive throne to either technologist or humanist, because each is only half the man or woman, capable of delivering only half of what society needs, without the other. This year's conference demonstrates our drive to stay in the forefront of those institutions graduating professionals distinguished by both competence *and* conscience.

Bentley College has chosen the field of Computer Information Systems as an area of selected excellence—that is, one of several disciplines in which we claim or aspire to leadership regionally and even nationally. It is also one of those few fields which commands extraordinary resource commitment in such areas as faculty, hardware, educational software and so forth. We already have one of the largest departments of Computer Information Systems (in terms of full-time faculty) in the Northeast.

We graduate more CIS majors than any institution of higher education in the Commonwealth of Massachusetts. All Bentley undergraduates—of whatever major—take at least two computer courses, and the vast majority take more. Again, we could choose

*President, Bentley College

to graduate skillful data processing technicians. But rather, we strive to educate toward competence *and* consçience. Employers appear to give high marks to our academic computer program, judging by the competition for our graduates. Yet we know that some employers prize our students for their immediately useful technical knowledge more than for their broader education, which, nevertheless, may be even more advantageous to the employer in the long run. Still, we realize that the computer field poses some unique educational challenges that are not found in the more traditional and stable business disciplines.

It is trite but still true to assert that the rate of technological change in this field of knowledge is increasing. As we move deeper into computer technology, we note too the growing complexity of the computer field, as lines between technologies and between disciplines blur and cross. Simultaneous change and complexity produce what social scientists call "turbulence." This turbulence is both exhilirating, and, as too many of us know, often frustrating.

Choices must be made to manage this technology, to harness its awesome potential, and to avoid hazards threatening individuals, organizations, and societies. That management job will take people with a sense of values, and the courage to be profiled in the glare of public examination. Bentley College wants to educate *just those people*—competent computer information systems professionals able and willing to serve human values, on both the producer's and the user's side.

In the broadest sense, we want all our students to be computer literate. In such rapidly changing times, we cannot afford a widening education gap such that those who have the authority to make decisions lack the ability, and those with the ability, but no legitimate authority, become decision-makers by default. The German poet Goethe warns, "Nothing is more alarming than ignorance in action."

We—and most of you—have taken on an enormous educational challenge. This conference should help all of us do our jobs a little better despite the pell-mell race of computer technology. We are on hazzardous terrain and, as one reporter cautioned us, "No one has tried such a conference before." That makes our two days together all the more promising.

We seek to put more concrete meaning into our conference theme: "Managing Computer Technology: Values and Choices in Corporate and Public Policy," so that we, as educators at Bentley, can both perform our mission more ably and contribute to the quality of computer affairs management in the public and private sectors.

We seek new ideas, connections between old ideas, inspiration, methodology, reality testing, and—most important—a network of people who share our informed excitement about the importance of our task. I am optimistic as I see the talent dedicated to this conference. I wish you exciting learning and good fellowship in these few days of deliberations.

CHAPTER 1

Computers and Business: A Case of Ethical Overload

Joseph F. Coates*

In this paper, I will discuss three topics. The first concerns how one comes to understand the future consequences of a major new technology. Then I will briefly note one or two ethical themes, and finally I will illustrate some of the future implications of computer technology.

If one talks with the cognoscenti, which part of my work involves, and asks, "What is in the wind, what are the kinds of developments in our society that might have effects comparable to those of the electric light bulb or of the automobile?" two topics invariably pop to the surface. One is the development of computers and their kindred telecommunications technologies; the second is developments in molecular biology. Our interest is in the first—the revolution in computer and telecommunications technology. It is exciting to know that for one of those rare times in recent history—that is, the history of the last 400 years—we are participating in a revolution and that we can be effective actors in its impetus and direction. Our awareness makes it particularly appropriate to think about the long-term ethical and moral implications of this technology as it moves into society.

In trying to understand the implications of a new technology there are three avenues to follow, three paths that will reveal what

*President, J. F. Coates, Inc.

the potentially important consequences are. The first is to look at the technology itself: It will have effects just as anything we do—where we locate things and how we organize our affairs—will affect the environment. Any technology therefore has direct effects simply because it is itself physical and is located and produced somewhere. Looking at the technology itself is one important way to foresee its consequences. Still more revealing is the second path—the one that looks at substitution. No technology is introduced entirely on its own merits; every technology is introduced because it does something that we already do in a way that is cheaper, faster, or better by some standard. By viewing new technology as substitution, one has a clue about two sets of effects—namely, the effect of the substitution itself (efficiency, lower cost, and so forth) and the effect on what it is being substituted for. We wipe out some old functions when we introduce new ones. The third, and most significant, avenue for getting at future consequences entails the examination of capabilities. Curiously enough, this examination is outside the usual scope of the entrepreneur businessman's argument for buying new technology. Every new and exciting technology, just because it is exciting, entails additional capabilities, capabilities that are often obscure until that technology is cheap and commonplace. It is on new capabilities that one should focus to understand the future implications of a major technology.

I will illustrate how we might have followed these approaches with a very common example, the automobile. Looking first at the technology alone, the automobile has affected the development of resources such as iron, steel, chemicals, and oil. It has affected manufacturing, the highway system, our death rates, and even the air that we breathe.

Viewing the automobile as a form of substitution, we see other significant effects. As a substitute for the horse and wagon, the automobile and truck solved the urban horse manure problem—a major environmental pollution and health problem in the early part of the century. Although it did away with that problem, in not too many years it had created new problems. By as early as 1915, the automobile had become an urban nuisance as well as a minor risk to safety.

We can see some even more interesting effects when we consider the special capabilities of the automobile. It brought us portable privacy, and that portable privacy has replaced some uses of the living room, the front porch, and the hayloft. Let me suggest how curious and real that privacy is. If you are stopped at a traffic light and look around, about 10 percent of the people in the cars will be picking their noses, and you know *that* is privacy. The car's portable privacy gives a profound sense of isolation. The car can also dissociate where you live from where you work. This capability has had major effects on land use and land use planning. It has led to the development of suburbia and to the end of living over the store.

These are then three paths to anticipating the consequences of a technology. Before following them to look at computers and the kindred technologies, let me pause for a moment to make a few observations about why it is important to consider business ethics in relation to this revolutionary new technology. My basic position is that we have reached the limits of the personal ethics of the Judeo-Christian tradition. It is just an absolute bust in providing any kind of moral guidance to any serious person in a complex community, in an institution, in a school, or in a corporation. There is no strong positive ethical culture in the American business community today. The standard ethical values echoed in the business community are the milksop banalities of a semisecularized ideology, Christianity. And the psychosocial, conversational chitchat approach of secularized Judaism is no better. Those who would enjoy a monopoly on ethical thought through organized religion have no ethical perspective beyond personalism. The consequence of this is that in an increasingly complex world the individual cannot ethically cope. We have to have some way of getting past the half-understood, half-remembered Sunday school lessons that corporate entrepreneurs, chief executive officers, and others tout so tediously. We have moved into a molecular world; their thinking is still atomic. Corporate ethics is an intellectual wasteland and a spiritual desert.

The mentality of the zero-sum game is really the only functioning ethic of the American corporate world. Everything is in conflict with everything else. I win, you lose. You win, I lose. We win, they lose. The day-to-day activities of a corporate executive are essentially a perpetual zero-sum game which fosters a perpetual adversarial view. This renders us unable to cooperate when cooperation is what is required by complexity. The predominant worldview of corporate senior officials—the graduates of MIT, Harvard, Cal Tech, or the University of Illinois, the children of the Depression, the products of World War II—is one focused on bigger, better, sooner, and faster. In their view, nature is fundamentally a bitch and the only way to deal with her is to beat her to her knees. Their choice of entertainment is a surrogate zero-sum game: corporate executives mindlessly watch weekend football because that is the surrogate entertainment for their zero-sum world. The corporate apex of insight into complexity is microeconomic analysis—the economics of the household blown large. Their cost-benefit analysis is fundamentally a variation on zero sum. The absence of an ethic of the organization and a calculus of values are the two ethical themes highlighted for the remainder of my discussion of computers and kindred technologies.

The computer is not a single entity. Rather, it is a family of devices ranging all the way from what one calls a mainframe computer—the kind of giant multimillion-dollar apparatus used by the military in its early warning systems and by large corporations to handle accounting, management, and actuarial functions—to minicomputers and macrocomputers—the kinds of equipment you can buy at retail outlets—on down to hand calculators and those devices that, while not smaller, are in some sense more obscure, like the microprocessor—the brain on a chip. This is the range of technologies that we must consider when we talk about how the computer affects the business community and the future of business. It is not just the future implications of the mainframe monsters that we are dealing with; it is also those of the microprocessor. Even as we talk about "the effects of the computer on business," we are using an obsolescent framework, for it is not the computer or the family of computers that is in and of itself important. What is important is the fact that the computer is converging with telecommunications technology to create a whole new complex in our society, a complex that the French have labeled "telematics." Telematics is the broader and therefore far more appropriate framework in which to explore the implications this new family of things has for society. I will therefore try to use the terms interchangeably, emphasizing computers where appropriate.

It is difficult to circumscribe the discussion because in talking about computers we are talking about a revolution, and just because the computer is revolutionary, it is going to affect everything we do. To get a sense of the scope of the changes, consider the range of effects of telematics: it will deal with information, affect everything that deals with information, affect everything that deals with knowledge, affect everything that deals with data, affect everything that deals with control mechanisms, affect everything that deals with analysis, affect everything that deals with memory, and affect everything that deals with feedback. In other words, telematics will affect all the functions that make up the bulk of our daily lives—remembering, storing, acquiring, recalling, controlling, and influencing. Certainly these are the central tasks in any well-managed corporation. The computer and its family of technologies will thus affect a corporation in all its aspects.

Let's begin with some of the capabilities implicit in technologies such as the minicomputer, the microprocessor, and kindred devices by considering a current energy problem—its rising cost. There is tremendous pressure to conserve and to be more efficient in what we do. Right now it is possible to place a device costing perhaps $50 to $125 on the junction box of your home that will provide you, the homeowner, with complete control over the use of every energy function in your house, enabling you to: keep Aunt Millie's room always at 80°; shut off the rest of the heating system until 4:30 in the afternoon; flip it on when you have dinner guests so that it rises to 72°; turn on the stove; and so forth. You can thus schedule the operation of your house as a function of multiple variables: the time of day, the cost of fuel, the things you are doing, and so on. Why don't we have this device? We don't have it simply because the business community is structured so that it is in no one's interest to produce it.

Although all of the analysis tells us that the real leverage in controlling energy is on the demand side, the utilities are concerned with supply; they are virtually addicted to supply-side solutions. Not seeing themselves in the business of managing demand, the utilities pass off demand technologies as consumer products. But, if you buy the control device as a consumer product—which, in fact, you can—you get one tenth the function at three times the cost. A fundamental problem with this new control technology is how to institutionalize it.

Consider, for example, the word processor. The word processor is an example of an applied computational technology, a memory-storage device with the ability to use information, to feed it back, and to store it. The word processor is beginning to revolutionize the office, but it is only beginning. Combine the concept of the word processor with what is right over the horizon, the morpheme generator invented by Texas Instruments, and we will get some very exciting developments. A morpheme is the basic unit of speech. Put phonemes together and you have morphemes; put morphemes together and you have speech. Texas Instruments put them together to develop a $20 chip that will synthesize the human voice. They first marketed it as a Christmas toy called "Speak and Spell." Just think of what it will be like when every device that we encounter can talk back: "Charlie, that's the first time you have ever spelled a word with three l's in a row." "Mary, we have searched your 450,000 word vocabulary, and that's a new spelling." Imagine a talk-back tax form: "Mr. Smith, did you really check box WZ34, and is that arithmetic correct?" "Do you wish to claim 34 children, or is that your wife's age?" Just think of the possibilities for the talking-back device: You are riding down the road. You see something beautiful, awesome, spectacular, unfamiliar, or curious. What the devil is it? Press the interrogator button on the dashboard, and the highway will talk back to you. You want the five-second interrogation. "On your right is so and so; on your left is such and such." You ask for 30 seconds worth. Oh boy, that was great. You park; you want the full four minutes. Just think how devices such as these might affect your world. If you drive, every year you spend on the average one full day of your life waiting to make left-hand turns. Calculate it: you actually do spend a day a year waiting to make left turns. Now, it is fully within the state of the art to have those intersections respond to the pressure or absence of traffic. That is what computation and control can do.

Think how these developments might affect the credit card. The French are now marketing a credit card with a brain on the chip that can be loaded. "Don't buy anything that comes from such and such a store." "You do not have any credit in this region." "This card is good up to a certain limit." When your card has a brain on a chip you, the entrepreneur, and the salesman now can interact on a whole new level.

Or take a set of serious medical problems. Take the case of a male who, as a result of a severe back injury to the lower spine, has become impotent. A brain on a chip can now provide him with a penile erection. Just press a button and zap, his hydraulic system is up and running.

Ultimately there is nothing in our lives involving control and feedback that is not going to be affected by telematics. That is why the business community and its ethical approach is so pallid. That is why it is so dull, so uninteresting; business is hawking all this stuff, just like Texas Instruments did, as Christmas specials. Immediacy and return on investment dominate corporate policy.

The microprocessor will be everywhere; it will touch everything we are concerned with. Let me illustrate with one more example of how we are losing out on the potential of this technology. If we stood on the roof, we could probably see the Polaroid Company within hailing distance of us. Edwin Land is one of the true inventive geniuses in America. He spent almost a third of a billion dollars on something called the SX 70. Although it was, in fact, a market bust, it is a fascinating device. There are a dozen technological *tours de force* contained in that little camera, twenty inventions, any one of which any inventor would be proud to call his own. And what is it? It is a toy. You and I could go through our lives without ever encountering an SX 70 and not even miss it. A third of a billion dollars.

Consider for a moment your orbit of first- and second-degree relatives—parents, siblings, uncles, aunts, grandparents, cousins, nephews, nieces. How many of you have a handicapped relative within that orbit? About two thirds. That is typical of a cross-section of an American middle-class group. That is typical, but you absolutely never would have guessed it on the basis of any public or private policy, or on the basis of any corporate action in America. Yet the problems of the handicapped are problems of input, of output, or of central processing. They are the problems of the language of the computer and feedback. They are the problems that contemporary science and technology, on its most exciting leading edge of development, is addressing. Yet two thirds of you have relatives suffering input, output, or central processing problems, and nobody—no Edwin Land, no IBM, no government agency—is doing very much to help them. Why? Because there is no conceivable way to make money from it: technology for the handicapped is an enormous market failure in America. Anyone like Edwin Land who turned his genius, his twenty marvelous inventions, to deal with the problems of the handicapped would take a bath. And the market and moral structure of our society is such that we have no way of drawing him out of the bath. Our society is increasingly plagued by problems of that sort—capabilities which cannot be brought to fruition through the market mechanism. Just think, two thirds of you have relatives who are suffering from that market failure.

Let us talk about a capability in addition to monitoring and feedback that this technology provides—the ability to dissociate work from the workplace. Most of you grew up cherishing the thought of going to some highrise factory in the middle of Boston, New York, Chicago, or heaven knows where. Every office building is really a simulation of the factory. Historically the office building grew up dependent on the factory. White collar work was dependent on the factory. But why did one go to the factory in the first place? Because an entrepreneur bought a large piece of equipment that would not fit in a cottage. The factory work had to come to the equipment, and white collar workers just followed along in traditional mimicry. That is now obsolete. There is virtually no function that is now performed in white-collar factory warrens that requires workers to be there. With the assistance of telematics, computers, microcomputers, and the brain on a chip, it can all be done elsewhere. Most paper work can be dispersed to suburban locations or even into the home. This development is going to create problems for the business community because our entire legal, institutional, and corporate structures are built around the framework of the factory and industrial society. Twenty years of civil rights legislation now makes it possible for the handicapped, for women, for blacks, Chicanos, and for all other groups to have access to jobs. But they are factory jobs. How can access to a facility employing twelve people, four people, or even one person be monitored? As telecommunications technology makes it possible to separate work from the workplace, corporate America will try to reinstitute the unfair system that we have just overcome. If the company does not like incompetent Blacks or inept Chicanos turned out by urban school systems, the business will, in the name of the organization's needs, use computer technology to employ literate, pliable, white working women to work at home. There are enormous equity questions associated with this technology.

The microcomputer at home or elsewhere is also a marvelously democratizing device. Those keys do not care anything about race, religion, national origin, or anything connected with the fingers that use them. An interesting twist that may evolve is the development of the intellectual sweatshop. An employee may play Tom Sawyer and have his or her children perform the tasks, or have a neighbor come in and do the task for a third of the wage. Even more horrendous is the control mechanism that might go along with it, namely, a sensor that says because we have our Mary Smith smell detector, or because we have our Mary Smith fingerprint readout that says it is Mary Smith's fingers tapping the keys, this machine is being operated by Mary Smith and by no one else. No matter how you look at it, it is trouble. The managerial control potentially residing in this technology is going to revolutionize industry, and the laggards are going to find themselves far behind. But worse than that, the business community is doing absolutely nothing to mediate this revolutionary dissociation of work from the workplace. The structure of American communities is such that codes, tax structures, and everything else work against, not for, this new movement in our society.

The third capability that comes with computers is the ability to completely dissociate tasks from the calendar and the clock. There is no reason why any white collar function has to be performed at 11:03 A.M. or 11:03 P.M., 6:04 A.M., or 6:04 P.M. Now we can do anything, or almost anything, at any time of the day or night. The home computer, tied to a mainframe computer connected by cable or satellite, permits you to perform almost any function during the whole day. It permits you to perform that function any time, any place, and as effectively as if you were under the supervisor's eye. Although we are truly moving into an around-the-clock society, corporate America has been unimaginative and foot dragging about the implications of this development. In fact, there is barely any discusison of it at all.

Computer technology will broaden the base of decision making while it simultaneously broadens the base of decision makers. The chain of command is broken. There is no need for a chain of command when the people down the line may have: (a) better knowledge, (b) greater responsibility, or (c) a greater stake in the decisions than anyone higher on the chain of command. Computer technology now makes it possible to introduce everyone in the chain into the process of decision making. More avant-garde companies will adapt; the laggards will resist and go the way of Chrysler.

Why do I keep emphasizing white collar workers? Simply because the main commodity in America today is information. Fifty-five percent of the work force is employed in the information business. America is no longer a society where products such as coal, oil, automobiles, steel, grain, farm, or manufactured goods predominate. Information and knowledge—knowledge generation and handling—are the dominant aspects of American society. A fundamental dissonance in our society today is that corporations are still structured around the industrial model. That model must be broken if not destroyed.

In promoting individual autonomy, computers are probably the single most important device to come down the pike since the printed word. A recent study suggests that among people who bought a "personal computer" for use at home, few were using it for any of the trivial reasons for which it is advertised. They were not putting their culinary information on the computer; they were not making it a calendar; they were not balancing their checkbooks, or whatever. If you can afford to buy a micro, you can balance a checkbook in the old way. These people were using their computers for one thing only—to achieve autonomy. Even professional computer programmers were running home from the factory, that hellhole for so many, called corporate America, to enjoy and play with their micros, to gain a sense of accomplishment. A man who had dropped out of school because he could not cope with calculus taught himself on the micro. With the computer, he achieved such a sense of autonomy and accomplishment, such a sense of fulfillment, that he wanted to buy one for each of his children. That is autonomy—one of the key value changes in society—and that is what the computer makes possible.

But what does this mean for business ethics? It means the top-down, zero-sum, nature-is-a-bitch, I-win-you-lose philosophy is rapidly becoming obsolete because you cannot run an operation that way with autonomous workers, and you certainly cannot run an information-based factory with anything but autonomous workers.

Another capability that the computer provides has to do with production. American business is fundamentally focused on producing, storing, delivering, and packaging. Inventory is a big problem in the business world, and inventorying will soon be dealt with through electronic warehousing. Why do we make so many things? We make things to meet uncertain demand, or to appeal to different market interests. As we robotize our factories, we will shrink that process. We will be able to order up and to tailor on demand any product that is wanted. This capability could completely reorder the production cycle. What the robotization of American industry implies is a renaissance of diversity, a renaissance in accomplishment, in invention, and in innovation.

Robots are now, to use the jargon of that industry, in their third generation. The first generation machinery performed highly complex, fixed tasks—often, if not usually, multiple tasks—on an assembly line or in a manufacturing process. Typically, first-generation robotization was a big step forward. The severe limitation on the first stage was that while the investments were big, the equipment was more or less fixed in function. Second generation robots are the "reprogrammables"—devices or machines that can be set to do one task and, when that task is done, can be reprogrammed to do a similar or even a strikingly different task. The new, or third, generation of robots reflects a substantial improvement in flexibility and adds a new element, sensing: to be able to check parts, to be aware of the orientation of equipment, is to acquire some of the additional skills of a human operator, namely, to respond to a changing environment and not merely to a fixed and predetermined situation. The second and third generations of robots often have been introduced into factories to deal with occupational health and safety requirements. For example, it turns out to be cheaper to robotize the painting of an automobile or the removal of castings from molds in a foundry, and both jobs involve highly polluted and dangerous atmospheres. However, the current movement toward robotization is driven by different considerations than worker safety. National and international competition and the search for productivity improvements are the primary drivers. This is where the new serious problem of business ethics occurs. Each entrepreneur is concerned, as he rightly should be, with his own self-interest. Each factory, each band of stockholders, each company may acquire some increment in productivity by robotization. But, questions of the effects on workers—of displaced workers, of migration

of jobs, of the impact of putting people and machines in closer prox-
imity—are issues that need public discussion and the development
of a new business ethics. Yet we have virtually no mechanisms for
that discussion.

An interesting sidelight on the problems of the use of computers
and telecommunications in business and industry comes about
through understanding the pathologies of the system. Perhaps the
most unequivocal pathology of many of these systems is theft.
Consider also the potential in our computerized society for destruction and sabotage. At home and in over a hundred countries in the
world, some elements of American society have pernicious, unjusti-
fied, evil, unwanted, undesirable, foul, and unacceptable impacts.
As a result there are people who do not care for us. They now, for
the first time, have a substantial opportunity to get back at us. A
bomb exploded in a University of Michigan computer room is kid's
stuff, infantile, compared to what the future holds. Just take the
case of electronic funds transfer (EFT). Industry, IBM, the banking
community, and regulators are working hammer and tong for bigger, better, sooner, faster. Let's suppose that $50 billion a day will
flush back and forth across America in the form of electrons. You
cannot find a quarter-inch-thick sheaf of discussion by any of those
connected with these entrepreneurial systems—customers, regulators, or vendors—describing the cost schedule that relates vulner-
ability to the risks. And what are the risks? The risks are incredible
just because nobody who can build a system capable of flushing
$50 billion across the country can understand the process by which
it is accomplished. The fundamental fact, and a fact of crucial importance to business in America, is that no one who designs, builds,
or maintains a complex system understands what it can do. Builders
understand very well what it is designed to do, but they do not understand what it *can* do. So a group of highschool boys in New
York, at the Dalton School, crack into a business computer in
Canada and bollix up the records. Are those boys sent to reform
school? No, because the very thought of taking them to court and
revealing how they did it is hair raising. A few years ago kids in
England played a counter-technology game: pick up the telephone,
call around the world, don't pay any money. They called around
the world with the maximum number of linkages—London, Edin-
burgh, Paris, Bern, Madrid, Rome, Ankara, Kabal, on to Delhi,
Tokyo, and back to Singapore, on and on, around the world, all the
way back to London. The final goal was to ring up in the next phone
booth for free. When they were caught, they were given amnesty in
exchange for telling how they did it. They were given amnesty

because the folks who sell and operate this technology could not answer the question of what the technology could do. That is the model of technology and computers in American business. That is the most important thing I have to tell you today.

The capabilities of computers to aggregate information will give us a new view of the world, a new sense of how the world operates and is structured. We get a little foretaste of this with the waves of epidemiological information that wash over us. We hear that contraceptive pills cause phlebitis, drinking coffee causes pancreatitis, and so on. All of this is a result of computer technology and its ability to scan 225 million people and to pick out effects that are occurring among five or 500 of them. Its capability in the future will be to find those five or 500 at an early stage and to treat them. The combination of the ability to aggregate, to analyze, and to feed information back will completely change the amount of epidemiological data that we collect and the level at which we address the problem of diseases in our society.

The capability to aggregate and to disperse information will, however, also create a problem for the business community. Now every time people discover that a company has done something wrong, the company has only one response: "those bastards, they're doing it again—they're out to get us." And yet, that is not necessarily the case. No one ever thought that the people who manufactured contraceptive pills were manufacturing phlebitis. Yet when the facts became clear, what do zero-sum addicts do? They deny it. They fight it. They have no sense that there is a problem they must deal with. The only common behavioral models for problem solution in corporate America are Chrysler and the Hooker Chemical Company—head in the sand, dumb denial. These are the only common models that corporate America has for responding to social issues—deny that there is a problem and fight like hell when they catch you. There are going to be more and more problems in the future, not fewer. Corporate America is going to have to devise better ways of dealing with them.

Let me illustrate what I mean. Minamata disease gained worldwide notoriety when it was acknowledged that Japanese fishing families were developing neurological disorders from eating fish contaminated by mercury dumped by a local company into the fishing waters of the bay. Industry denied it; public health people denied it. It took about ten years until, finally, everyone said, yes, it is the mercury. The company then said they were causing the problem and said they would stop. Now, anyone in the world who uses mercury knows about Minamata disease, and anyone tuned into environmental problems knows about it. In August of 1981 the U.S. Government's Center for Disease Control in Atlanta announced that an American multinational corporation has been dumping mercury, in quantities that are beyond belief, into Lake Managua in Nicaragua. They had dumped not ounces, not pounds, but tons. And when Nicaraguans justifiably say that they must work out their vengeance on the villains, considerable repercussions can be expected.

The capabilities of computers and computer technologies are such that they must change our language. There is no question but that the technology of symbols is rapidly changing. For the first time, computer technologies permit us to approach the world with holistic, integrated models. They permit us to look at and to think about things literally in new ways. Computer technologies get us off the path of linear thinking and onto the path of interactive thinking. We will develop a vocabulary and a language for using that capability, and that language will have major effects on what we do because it will affect the way we think.

But let me suggest some other minor, but potentially important, effects to which we are not paying attention. The hand calculator, smallest of the computers marketed as computers, is now used universally in schools of economics, engineering and science. Any engineer over thirty years old learned science on the basis of two concepts. First he learned to understand the theory, to think in theoretical terms, and to do rough calculation; then he learned to conduct detailed quantitative analysis. And he learned the two skills in an interactive way. Now, without ever questioning how it might affect his or her ability to think, we give the freshman engineer a device that can instantly carry calculations to four or five decimals. We have thus introduced a fundamental change in the student's intellectual furnishings. The same is true for economists. That ability to calculate to the fourth decimal may be deceiving; it may lead you to believe that you know what you are doing, when in fact you may be obscuring real understanding. You see this kind of problem even at the elementary school level where children are given $5 calculators. What is the first three years of school devoted to? Learning two things: the rudiments of reading and four arithmetic functions—adding, subtracting, multiplying, and dividing. Three years can now be compressed into six months. And what are they doing for the remaining two-and-a-half years? Nothing, absolutely nothing. There is no innovation, no imagination, only further alienation of new generations of students from that potentially exciting process called education.

What does computation imply for education? Along with telematics, it means that, for the first time, we can achieve three of the long-term goals of educators. Tied to telecommunications technology, computational technology now permits true mass education. It permits true individualized education, and it permits true, honest-to-goodness, lifelong education. It permits us to deliver any message to a mass of people or to deliver a specific tailored message to you, when and where you want it.

What does this capability mean for corporate America and its ethics? It means that there will be a changed relationship between corporate America and our other major social institution, education; that business might not only become a potential competitor for education, but it might also be a source of its upgrading; and that business can potentially provide either a way of delivering enormous new benefits to its workers, or a means of social and intellectual control over them. When unions and professional workers recognize that their benefits package will include life-long education, we, as a society, shall have to make a moral choice about what to put into that package. It is unlikely that the average fifty-year-old senior executive, trained in morally obsolescent concepts, will have a socially responsible view about what this package should include.

This computational revolution, this telematics revolution, this movement to an information-and-knowledge-based society will have other interesting effects, effects with which corporate America will have a hard time coping. Let me suggest, as an example, a particular case. Hybrid corn is a successful commodity for two reasons. The first is an obvious one: it is a good product; hybrid varieties really provide better, cheaper corn. But that is not a sufficient reason for its success. The exciting aspect of hybrid corn is that, since hybrid corn is not self-propagating, the farmer must go back to a hybridizer every year for seed, and there is a built-in incentive for the hybridizer to continually improve the quality of his product. This strong tie to profit is not characteristic of self-propagating crops. One might anticipate that if we could get this kind of a feedback system, into the development of other foods and grain, we could revolutionize food production. Perhaps we can, because every plant is nothing more than the embodiment of its genetic code. Every living thing—you, me, and a blade of grass—are nothing more than the embodiment of a message, a genetic message that, in principle, can be read. When we can read that message, we will be able to introduce a royalty system into self-propagating grain and vegetable products, and hence revolutionize agricultural production. Picture a carload of wheat coming up to General Mills. Sample a pint of it. Run it through the DNA analyzer—30 percent Smith variety, 40 percent Brown variety, the rest mixed and unknown. Now, you can have a royalty system to pay Smith and Brown. This possibility should provide a sense of the enormity of the revolution entailed in combining computational technologies with the other capabilities that we have.

It is with that sense of what the future may hold with respect to computers and kindred things that I shall stop. To sum up, the new immorality is to choose to act in ignorance.

Discussion

Question: What are the substitution impacts of automation? Will workers be replaced, for example?

Coates: The question is not, "Will workers be displaced?" but "What will happen to them?" And let me suggest several of the things that will happen. One is that jobs will be upgraded. These machines don't really operate themselves. The factory assembly-line drudges will be replaced by people who have a more interesting level of work. Some people say you will replace one and a half for two. Take any number you want; a substantial percentage will be replaced but by no means all.

The second effect on the worker is that it will further blur the already blurring line between white- and blue-collar work. You may, in fact, be able to introduce new diversity into the robotized factory simply because the nature of the work will muddy that distinction. The functions will no longer be as clear as they are now.

A third exciting thing happening with the computational and telematics revolution is that the old factory or industrial model of the distinction between work and leisure is beginning to fade. I anticipate that more, rather than fewer, nonwork activities will be assimilated into the work place.

We now have a nonwork activity in the form of a coffee break. We have a nonwork activity in the form of United Fund collections. All kinds of nonwork activities now occur at the workplace, and we can anticipate that they will increase. As productivity goes up, we'll have more latitude with the choices.

Another thing to keep in mind about displaced workers is the question of why you work forty hours a week. You work forty hours a week, typically, because you're a forty-five-year-old white male with a parent, a grandparent, three kids, and a wife to support.

But there are very few people who need to do that any more. Only about 7 percent of Americans live in a *Saturday Evening Post*-cover family. Increasingly, women are going to work, and increasingly, women are getting jobs on a parity with men. Soon it will come to the point where we don't even have to make gender distinctions; we'll talk about working couples, dual-income families.

That's the first wave. But quickly society will learn that you don't have to work those forty hours, that you can share jobs, split jobs; you can take three months off, you can have six months off. You have a whole new kind of freedom in your choices about work. I think that this phenomenon will absorb some of the surplus labor created by the telematics revolution. Because the fact is that we're moving into a society in which families are on parity, dual-income earners.

Question: Originally you were pessimistic about the behavior of corporate America; now you seem to be optimistic about the changing nature of the work force. Is there a contradiction here?

Coates: Let me elaborate on that. First of all, keep in mind that everything is going to happen. We're going through an enormously exciting time during which there is a great deal going on. The more advanced companies will promote arrangements that will encourage split worktime families; they will accommodate part-time workers; they will accept the three-month sabbatical. Why? Because there's always somebody who is avant garde or in the lead. The Chryslers of the world, the mass of corporate America, will slide into a kind of corporate senescence.

Question: You suggested previously that there is no commitment on the part of computer companies to helping the handicapped. There are several businesses which are interested, for example, in helping the blind, and which have highly skilled blind people working for them, however. So there obviously is some demand on the computer industry to make computer technology acceptable to these people.

Coates: What you're saying is absolutely correct. But the examples you allude to are inconsequential, trivial, totally incommensurable with the size of the problem. Fly on any airline, and open the slick magazine they give you. Every other page has an ad for a word processor, a microcomputer, or some kind of device that none of you really need. But you can't open a national magazine, or even a specialized magazine, and find an ad for an absolutely new whiz-bang hearing aid, or a great development for someone who's spastic, or a new joint development for your uncle who lost his knee in 1945.

What you're describing is absolutely correct but socially trivial compared with the capabilities used to produce office equipment. No matter how you slice it, failure to produce in the area you mentioned is an intrinsic failure of the marketing system. That's the point I want to drive home. The situation with the handicapped is not unique. There are other things we can't do, because the market system doesn't permit it.

Let me illustrate. It happens to be off the mark, but I wouldn't want you to think that it was only computers and manufacturers which reflect systemic failure. Right now, we're about to have an earthquake in San Francisco—in five years, six years, eight years, who knows? But the city is going to fall.

We're about to develop an earthquake prediction technology, incidentally dependent on the ability of computers to analyze seismographic data. Let's assume that before the quake comes, we have in place a credible predictive capability of 90-percent probability. What would corporate America do if this occurred? Bleed California dry overnight, get the money out instantly. That was discovered in an analysis that the Federal Emergency Management Agency sponsored three years ago. This presents a very interesting ethical problem. There is absolutely no way now in the United States to deal with what everyone familiar with the problem recognizes as a near certainty—an earthquake disaster. And a credible earthquake prediction system would drain all the money out of California at the very time that money would be needed to hedge against the impending disaster.

Question: Earlier this morning you were talking about the fact that computer technology will allow a lot of white-collar functions to be done outside the office. There are some people who say, on the other hand, that what will happen is that managers and professionals will, with technology, have more time to use their interpersonal skills interacting with people, where their expertise really is felt to be.

Coates: I reject that altogether. It's a corporate fancy to think that the average middle manager or senior manager has some enormous, latent bundle of capabilities which, if understood, would make him a whiz kid. The fact is, he's a fairly competent drudge. And the real fear is that this technology is going to wipe him off the scene.

Question: At the beginning of your talk you appeared to give short shrift to the abilities of the Judeo-Christian ethical code to address itself to the problems you're talking about. There's a plethora of activity both in religious and other circles, and scholars have addressed these problems. There are business ethics courses, seminars, symposia such as this one....

Coates: The simple fact is that I think you're wrong. For example, read this book by Sissela Bok on lying. *The New York Times* reviewed it, *The New York Review of Books* reviewed it, *The Atlantic* reviewed it, and everybody says the Bok book is the greatest thing to come down the pike. In my view it is ethically trivial, an exercise in high-class casuistry, and anyone in corporate America confronted with any of the problems that I've presented to you today would find Bok's book useless.

But let me give you an example of what I mean, and how the absence of anything in the Judeo-Christian tradition commensurate with the problem yields ethical pathologies. Your company is producing an automobile, you know it has a defect in it, and you know it's going to cost four and a half cents to fix the defect. But, if you fix it, it's going to cost the company two million dollars in revenue. So, what do you do? There's nothing you can do. Internally, you are told to talk to the manager, present it through the grievance mechanism, do it like a professional. Which means, if you proceed professionally once, you are ignored; if you do so twice, you're a pariah; if you do it three times—you're fired.

There's no mechanism for dealing with this sort of problem in corporate America. Ralph Nader's way of dealing with it is a perversion: rat on them, squeal, go public.

There's something wrong with a system which gives you only two choices: be a fink, or be ineffective. These are essentially the limits of moral thinking in corporate America.

I think that what you find is a lot of mushmouthed jabbering in the form of so-called discussions about corporate ethics, but nothing that really represents either an understanding of the situation or anything which is actionable.

CHAPTER 2

Computer Technology and Human Values

The Promise and Problems of Computer Technology

*James C. Emery**

By any reasonable standard, computer technology has been fantastically successful. Since the dawn of the electronic computer age in the mid-1940s, the raw speed of computers has increased by a factor of perhaps ten million, and the cost of a given computational task has gone down by a factor of as much as ten thousand. In that short span of time the computer industry has become one of the major economic, political, and military forces in the world. Few organizations have been untouched by these advances, and it is becoming increasingly evident that our personal lives will be similarly affected. The computer lies at the core of the emerging Information Age; it has become the very symbol of an advanced technological society.

RISKS OF THE COMPUTER AGE

Not surprisingly, such an unprecedented rate of development has brought with it a number of problems. The computer is viewed by many with decidedly mixed feelings: with great awe, but also with considerable hostility. The computer has a reputation—often deserved—of being intimidating, unfriendly, and unforgiv-

*Wharton School, University of Pennsylvania

ing. It has become a widely used scapegoat for errors, unemployment, and the frustrations of living in an uncaring mass society. It is feared as a potential tool of despots and an instrument for wholesale crime at microsecond speed.

These fears are not without justification. Because it is such a powerful tool, the computer has vast potential for good or evil; our experience to date provides many examples of both. We are a long way from understanding how best to protect ourselves from computer abuses.

Much of the attention on this issue has focused on the prevention and detection of computer-based crime. As more and more of our commerce is transferred to computer systems, our exposure to such crime grows very rapidly. Literally billions of dollars a day are moved about the world at startling speeds, with scarcely a trace except for electronic pulses and magnetic spots. This provides an inviting target for organized crime and an irresistible temptation for amoral computer "hackers." It is an open question whether our ever-improving methodologies for preventing and detecting computer crime can stay sufficiently ahead of the thief to thwart competent and determined efforts to penetrate our systems.

Another problem that has received well-deserved attention is the risk that computer-based systems may jeopardize personal privacy. This risk becomes all the greater as the volume of machine-readable data grows and as advances in technology make it easier to exchange information among previously fragmented systems. In this environment, we must be extremely wary of political abuses of personal liberty, as well as of insensitive misuses of personal data for commercial or bureaucratic purposes.

While I would not wish to minimize the vast mischief that may be caused by computer crime and the abuse of privacy, to my mind the greatest burden in the computer age comes not from the competent malefactor; it comes, rather, from the well-intentioned but incompetent designer of bad systems. In terms of their cumulative cost to society and the individual, mediocre systems that fail to exploit the power of the technology are the greatest and most persistent hazard we face. We all pay a tremendous price for error-prone, inflexible, unimaginative, and insensitive systems: we pay every time we get an erroneous (and uncorrectable) bill from the department store, when we must pore through reams of paper to find a nugget of useful information, when we must write essentially the same information five times when we register for a university course, when it takes six months to get a simple change made in a report, or when we have to wait three weeks to get a routine, out-of-stock item.

PROBLEMS AND REMEDIES

We don't *have* to design bad systems. The technology and methodology are at hand to deliver far better systems than we typically find. In order to implement an effective system, we should recognize some of the more common problems and apply the remedies that have proven successful in a variety of situations.

A common problem is the failure to recognize the great complexity of a comprehensive management information system (MIS). But the complexity of an MIS does not mean that it cannot be implemented. It just means that we must develop the system with great care, using a disciplined engineering methodology. The cost of such management is not insignificant—that is one of the reasons it is often not done very well—but it almost always pays big dividends.

Many of the systems developed today fail to exploit available technology. This is not surprising, in view of the rapid rate of change that has taken place, but we pay a substantial penalty for this inertia. We now have available to us a variety of highly productive tools that make it possible to develop a system in a fraction of the time and cost required using more conventional methodology. Among the more important tools are data base management systems, inquiring languages, report writers, and screen formatters. A developer of a new system who does not take advantage of such tools is probably making a serious mistake. (Retrofitting an old system to take advantage of current technology is another story; it is often like putting a jet engine in a Model T.)

Some system designers make just the opposite error, and attempt to go beyond well-tested technology. Being a pioneer in using new hardware, software, or methodology is generally risky. It should be avoided unless one can gain some compelling advantage, and even then it helps to have a big bankroll. A key to successful system design is knowing when to jump into a new development after it has been proven by the more adventurous or foolhardy.

Inflexibility is a common failing of many existing systems. A very widespread complaint of users is that it takes days and even weeks to get a seemingly trivial change made in a report or a processing task. Technicians, on the other hand, often complain that users can never make up their minds about what they want from the system. The remedy to this dual problem is, first of all, to recognize that change is inevitable; the only system that doesn't change is one that is not being used. Having recognized that flexibility is a design requirement, we can then take the appropriate technical steps to achieve a much higher degree of flexibility than most systems currently provide. This can be done through such means as the use of modular design, table-driven (parameterized) programs, good documentation, ad hoc inquiry languages, report writers, and data base management systems.

Perhaps the most damning criticism of information systems is that they fail to recognize the needs of users. Unsatisfied users include the president who has difficulty in understanding an obscure report, as well as the clerk who is put through mental contortions in order to correct a simple error. The deficiency may be one of omission rather than commission—when, for example, a system fails to relieve a user of a pesky, burdensome task that a well-designed system can handle as an easy by-product of its other chores. The remedy here is fairly obvious (although by no means universally applied): get users involved in systems implementation. An important first step is to educate users to be knowledgeable consumers of information and to be more sensitive to what a good information system should (and should not) do for them.

FUTURE PROSPECTS

Despite the well-known problems in our field, we can certainly point to some highly successful systems. A successful system is likely to provide interactive support for both clerical functions and management decision making; it is user-friendly, able to assist the user and cope with human errors; it is flexible and adaptable; and it strikes a good balance between the cost of the system and the benefits it provides.

Such systems are certainly feasible with today's technology, but they are not especially common. Much of this is due to the fact that most current systems were designed quite a few years ago, when the available technology and design methodology made it very difficult to implement a system that satisfies all of the goals that we now aspire to achieve. Distressingly enough, however, even newly implemented systems often fail to meet reasonable expectations. One can only conclude that success requires a relatively rare set of circumstances.

The development of a successful management information system is a large undertaking. It requires a long-term commitment on the part of an organization. It requires a disciplined approach to software engineering, with careful specification at each design stage and a formal method of scheduling and controlling all of the tasks required to develop an operational system. It requires a high level of technical and managerial skills on the part of the computer staff.

Some organizations will be able to put all of these together; many will not. Those that are successful are likely to reap substantial rewards in the form of improved efficiency and effectiveness, better product quality, and the ability to offer an impressive variety of attractive services to their clients. We are their clients, and our lives will be better for their success. Eventually the technology is likely to mature to the stage at which it can be implemented successfully by the average company that has only the average level of managerial and technical skill. In the meantime, we must face the prospect of continued frustrations in dealing with badly designed information systems—a situation made all the worse by the knowledge that it need not be so.

Chapter 2B

The Bias of Computer Technology

Weighing the costs against the benefits of computer technology is a subtle and exacting task. It is also exceedingly frustrating because the more urgent the need to secure the advantages and minimize the negative consequences of the technology, the more contentious becomes the discussion of issues. In part, this stems from lack of precision and specificity in the identification of costs and benefits. Costs and benefits may be realized over the long or the short term, they may vary from one group to another, and they may cast a shadow beyond the particular case being considered. For example, word-processing and file-management systems, components of office automation, have an immediate impact on the jobs of clerks and secretaries. In the longer term, these technologies will alter the functions of supervisory personnel and higher-level management, and will contribute to a fundamental restructuring of office operations. Table 1 shows some of the discriminations that must be made to identify costs and benefits of office automation to different groups over varying time periods.

The office automation example suggests that it is difficult, if not meaningless, to speak of one set of costs and benefits for society as a whole. More often than not, the term "society" is used to obscure the self-serving character of policy analyses (Mowshowitz, 1981).

*Croton Research Group, Inc.

Table 1. Possible Costs and Benefits of Office Automation

	Near-Term		Long-Term	
	Costs	Benefits	Costs	Benefits
Office workers	Layoffs Downgrading of skills Need to acquire new skills	More interesting work Elimination of some routine and boring jobs	Fewer jobs Tighter office discipline	New career paths for a select few
Managers	Implementation problems Personnel problems	Greater control over employees Improved information services	Fewer jobs for middle managers	Improved support for decision making
The organization	Increased expenditures on equipment Dislocations during implementation	Higher productivity More responsiveness	Unstable labor relations	Increased competitiveness Higher profits
Government	Higher unemployment payout	Modernization of nation's capital plant and equipment	Education and training for new skill requirements	Increased revenues

Closely related to the question of determining costs and benefits is the problem of distinguishing the consequences of computer technology from the effects of other phenomena associated with the introduction or use of that technology. One way of handling this problem is to distinguish between simple and complex effects of computer technology. Simple effects are very closely tied to the technology itself, exemplified by faster and more accurate techniques for obtaining numerical solutions to systems of differential equations. Simplicity here refers to the relationship of the observed phenomena to the computer—the more direct, the simpler.

An example of a complex effect is a change in organizational control structure resulting from the introduction of a management information system in a large company. Whereas simple effects are directly attributable to the computer, complex effects involve the computer as a catalyst, or perhaps as an occasion, for social change. These latter effects are aptly termed "complex" because of the human and social choices they comprise and involve. In cases of social change occasioned by computer technology, there are typically many possible and feasible ways of using computers, each of which may give rise to a different social arrangement.

A more subtle and diffuse impediment to cost-benefit analysis of computing lurks in the relationship of technology to social phenomena. The computer shares with other instruments ambiguities over modes of influence and social impact. Indeed, it is questionable whether it makes sense to speak of the "impact of computers on society" as if something called "computer" could collide with something called "society" (Laudon, 1974). Beyond the nuts, bolts, and semiconductors that make up the hardware, it is virtually impossible to isolate "pure technology" from "pure society." From conception to design to construction to implementation to use, computer systems involve social organization.

In addition to the logical fallacy of equating part with whole, the incommensurability of technology and society has implications for the argument that technology is purely instrumental in human affairs. Reduced to essentials, this argument asserts that computers as well as other devices are instruments that can be used for good or evil purposes, and that the choice of how these instruments are to be used is entirely free. I agree the computer is an instrument, but it is not a neutral instrument, since its use is socially and historically conditioned. There is no way to predict the consequences of computer use by looking solely at the potential of the technology to accomplish this, that, or the other. Social arrangements mediate between the things the technology is capable of supporting and the reality of the applications that ultimately emerge. Unless one realizes that computer technology is developed, anchored, applied, and used within social settings which have histories and traditions that constrain human choice, one cannot ascertain what is likely to happen and what effects this technology will have.

A simple analogy, often used to show the instrumental character of technology, compares the computer with a knife, which can be used by a surgeon to heal people or by an assassin to harm people. What is missing from this analogy is the social context in which instruments such as knives are introduced. No one in his right mind would distribute knives to madmen, but technical innovations are routinely distributed with very little concern for society's ability to make appropriate use of them. The notion of free choice in the use of an instrument suggests an idealized human being, one for whom decision making and choice are entirely unconstrained by society. Needless to say, no such animal exists. Individuals have interests and loyalties deriving from membership in groups and institutions. These interests and loyalties clearly play a significant role in determining the choices they make.

The diffusion of computer technology is subject to the same caveats as the distribution of knives. More complex instruments than knives necessarily render analysis more difficult. But it is clear that the particular uses to which computers are put depend on the social settings in which these devices are introduced, as well as the judgments of individuals confronted with the range of potential applications of the technology. Human and social dispositions figure prominently in the diffusion and shaping of new technology. Since these dispositions are characteristic of any social situation, technical instruments are not neutral; their uses reflect the character of the social settings in which they are found.

DIMENSIONS OF CHANGES ASSOCIATED WITH COMPUTERS

The title of this paper is adapted from a work by Harold Innis (1951), the late Canadian economist who attempted to show how media of communication have influenced social, political, and cultural development throughout history. Innis argued that media of communication—stone, papyrus, parchment, paper, radio, television—have unique characteristics which impress themselves on the social systems they help to support. For example, papyrus, because of its limited availability and centralized mode of production, contributed (along with an exceedingly complex method of writing) to the formation of a monopoly of knowledge in ancient Egypt presided over by the priesthood. By contrast, parchment, which was made from animal skins, supported the dispersed centers of knowledge of medieval Europe.

Innis derived the bias imparted by communication media to society almost exclusively from inherent characteristics of the media. According to Innis, a cultural focus on durable artifacts (e.g., stone tablets) emphasizes time and continuity, and lends itself to the development of religion rather than political administration and law. Lightweight and easily transported artifacts (such as paper) exert a bias in favor of the administration of territory.

Although I also claim that technology exhibits bias, I believe that bias is derived from two sources: from the inherent characteristics of particular technologies (as Innis argues), and from the dispositions of the social settings in which the technologies are introduced. The latter component of bias is especially apparent in the more complex cases such as information technology. The design and manufacture of microelectronic circuits requires a high degree of capital concentration, but the chips themselves, when mass produced, are flexible and inexpensive and can be used to support centralized or decentralized applications of computer communications. The one source of bias, inherent features, suggests economic concentration in the semiconductor industry; the other source, characteristics of social settings, gives a less clear reading but does point to hypotheses that warrant careful analysis.

The main point of the foregoing discussion is that the social history of computer use is not a random process. If there is a probability distribution over the range of potential uses of computers, it is very highly skewed by the two sources of bias identified above.

Despite the difficulties of assessing the costs and benefits of computer applications, decisions must be made and policies formulated that bear on the future of computers. Given this fact of life it behooves the student of social issues in computing to assist the decision maker and the policy planner to act in the best interests of as many groups and individuals as possible.

One way to assist is to provide guidelines for analyzing the effects of computer use. The first step is to identify the dimensions of changes associated with computers. Three fundamental dimensions of such changes are: time, mediation, and space. These three categories of analysis are self-explanatory except perhaps for mediation. Computer technology mediates changes directly when the observed changes are clearly attributable to the technology. Indirect mediation is characteristic of changes that result from modifications in social organization induced by computer use. Table 2 provides examples of each of the categories of changes. Although discrete subdivisions of the dimensions are shown, these are of course somewhat arbitrary—time, mediation, and space, each defines a continuum; the limitations of the observer dictate discrete subdivisions.

In what follows, I will be concerned primarily with long-term, indirect and diffuse kinds of changes which I term *systemic*.

Table 2. Dimensions of Changes Associated with Computer Technology

Dimension	Examples of Changes
Time	
Immediate	Introduction of numerically controlled system turns skilled machinist into machine monitor
Near-term	Unemployment, higher productivity
Long-term	New skills and training programs required for industry; growth or decline of a neighborhood
Mediation	
Direct	Modified practices such as result from replacing conventional typewriter by a word-processing system or a filing cabinet by a retrieval system
Indirect	Modes of human interaction or organizational arrangements altered after introduction of a management information system
Space	
Localized	Information flow in a particular organization altered by a time-sharing system with mailbox facility
Diffuse	National computer-communications network allows for electronic mail nationwide

NORMATIVE CHARACTER OF TECHNOLOGY ASSESSMENT

The exercise of assessing technology is a normative, as well as descriptive, enterprise; it is certainly not value free. This point warrants special emphasis in dealing with systemic effects because analysis is inescapably based on an interpretation of history. Insight into historical development is guided by empirical observations, but interpretation requires principles of both moral and analytical types which do not come from empirical observation. Values, attitudes, and expectations are integral parts of the assessor's kit. Cost-benefit analysis is strongly influenced by values and ideologies. How one will identify and weigh the costs and benefits of a particular technology depends very greatly on whether one subscribes to the idea of progress, to the ideology of class conflict, to the cyclical interpretation of history, or to another ideological position. Each view involves a number of assumptions and presuppositions which add distinctive coloration to respective assessments.

Why worry about the normative character of cost-benefit analysis? Although it is meaningless to speak of expunging values and ideologies from the assessment process, the analyst does have the choice of concealing biases (actively or passively) or making them as explicit as possible. The discussion of science and technology policy would contribute far more to public enlightenment than it does now if the latter course were routinely followed.

SOCIAL CONTROL: KEY TO SYSTEMIC EFFECTS OF COMPUTERS

Change in the forms and loci of social control is the key to understanding the systemic effects of computer technology. Any assessment of long-term costs and benefits of computers which ignores this element is doomed to irrelevance.

Questions of social control pervade all levels and forms of social organization: federal, state and local government; national organizations and local clubs; family and religious groups, and so forth. The function of social control is to preserve the integrity of social groupings. Political power, designed to maintain social stability in the nationstate, is one type of social control.

The principal link between computer technology and social control is through the technology's impact on social organization. Computers invite the restructuring of organizations through their promise of greater efficiency, flexibility, and effectiveness. Government agencies such as the Social Security Administration and the Federal Bureau of Investigation have created large computerized data bases to improve the administration of their programs and services. Private organizations such as banks, insurance companies, and manufacturers have introduced computer systems to improve the efficiency of their services, offer new services, or reduce the costs of producing goods and services. Each case involves some changes internal to the organization, as well as some external changes. Internal changes typically result in altered job definitions or modified supervisory relationships. External changes alter the relationship between consumers, clients, or citizens and the organizations which serve them.

These changes imply shifts in social control. Altered supervisory relationships signify direct shifts in social control. The implications of the substitution of a computerized payment system for Social Security checks are just as significant but more subtle. Looking beyond the proximal reasons for developing such a system, one sees a change in the form of dependency of retired persons on the Social Security Administration. This means that the bureaucracy has acquired new methods of monitoring and influencing the behavior of individuals. What is more, each service innovation of this kind adds to the social importance of the agency and thus enhances its power.

To fully appreciate the computer's relationship to social control, it is necessary to examine historical developments which reveal long-term shifts in the forms and loci of social control in Western society. The study of these shifts quickly leads one on a grand tour of Western history reaching back to the Middle Ages. At first glance it may seem far-fetched to connect, however tenuously, events of the Middle Ages with the computer, that most modern of modern inventions. Yet there is a connection: the computer, in its quintessentially modern roles, amplifies the effects of the transformation of society which signalled the decline of the medieval world.

Social control in the Middle Ages was based on status and membership in local groups, such as neighborhood, church, family, guild, and so forth (Nisbet, 1953). Group integrity was ensured by controls rooted in tradition and operating at a local level. All this has changed gradually but steadily over a very long period. Fueled by the rise of towns, a resurgence of commerce, the development of a market economy, and the emergence of a meritocratic officialdom, the transformation has shifted much of social control from the local group to the remote bureaucracy, and changed its mode of operation from personal suasion and small group pressure to the formal coercion of impersonal organizations.

These changes in the loci and forms of social control were the outgrowth of two closely related developments: (1) the rise of the nation state and (2) the weakening or dissolution of intermediate associations. The importance of these developments lies in the creation of a supreme sovereign authority within the nation. In the Middle Ages, organizations derived their legitimacy largely from tradition. The triumph of the state has essentially eliminated tradition as a source of legitimacy, replacing it with the formal charter of the sovereign authority. This change has profoundly weakened intermediate associations, and has created a kind of dual sovereignty: the individual, armed with inalienable rights endowed by natural law, versus the state, replete with security forces (von Gierke, 1900).

The weakening of associations that once provided individuals with services now furnished by government agencies lies at the heart of the shift in social control. Computer technology has served to reinforce and continue the shift through its use in information-processing applications in large bureaucracies. Such a consequence of the technology is not predictable from the range of potential uses of computers. It is, however, a very plausible outcome in view of inherent features of the technology combined with characteristics of the society in which computers have been used.

POLICY ISSUES IN PERSPECTIVE

The major policy issues surrounding the use of computers—jobs, work life, participation in decision making, economic growth, privacy, and so on—have, in various forms, been around for a long time. Indeed, the conditions that spawned these issues—mainly changes in methods of production—date from the industrial revolution. By pointing this out, I do not mean to belittle contemporary policy discussion, but to put the issues in perspective, and by so doing to extend the range of observation and experience that can be drawn upon to resolve them.

Although computer applications have put their own unique stamp on these issues, they are, nevertheless, recognizable from the past. Terminology has changed, specifics of social practices have changed, but the central problems have remained the same. Nineteenth-century observers worried about productivity, organizational change, and value shifts in the context of rapid industrialization. Attention in the late nineteenth and early twentieth centuries focused on mechanization associated with the assembly line and techniques of mass production. In the 1950s, the term "automation" found its way to center stage. More recently our penchant for new coinages has been unleashed in the search for an apt designation of persistent problems: cybernation, computerization, informatization, to name but a few.

What lies at the root of the naming game is varying perceptions of industrialization, urbanization, and related changes in the modern world. Major technological innovations have occurred in a world that has been shifting steadily from rural agrarian to urban industrial, from principalities of very limited power and means to nation states of undreamed of power and resources. In both the political and economic spheres, the modern world has produced the large organization—large-scale production units, mammoth bureaucracies for administering social programs, and so forth.

Historians have long argued about what constitutes the prime mover of history. Is it the singular individual who imposes his will on events, or is there something that might be termed an historical force that determines actions and events? This dispute will probably never be resolved (for long); it is instructive in the present context because it reflects an intellectual awareness of the complexities of social causation. Too often information policy questions are discussed as if they had no antecedents, and as if computer technology, in some pure, socially disembodied state, were a simple cause of social change.

Promoters of technological innovations may be forgiven hyperbole born of passionate belief in the wonders of something new. Policy analysts ought to know better. Computer technology did not father the idea of functional specialization, or of division of labor, or of the separation of control from task performance, or any number of other important concepts that figure so prominently in the design of computer systems. Indeed, the development of the ideas on which the computer is based mirror these earlier social and intellectual innovations.

The computer was introduced into a world of centralized organizations with a high degree of functional specialization. It is therefore hardly any wonder that computers and related communications devices serve as rationalizing instruments.

THE BIAS OF COMPUTERS

I believe that computer technology does have a bias, attributable, as explained above, to inherent features of the technology and to the social settings in which computers are developed and used. This bias can be seen in the types of computer-based products and services available, in the location of these products and services, and in their sources. Until very recently, computers were found almost exclusively in large organizations—big corporations, government agencies, universities, and so on. The computer industry has been and continues to be dominated by a handful of very large companies. Most computer applications are designed to increase productivity and efficiency or to reduce costs.

The elaborate infrastructure required to produce the technology, the control of its diffusion by elite groups, and the dominant role of large organizations in its use all point to a bias in favor of centralized social control. The growing market for microcomputers, despite appearances to the contrary, reinforces this view. Not very long ago personal computing enthusiasts predicted a mass market for stand-alone microcomputers, that is a market situation whereby tens of millions of American families would acquire personal computers. As it turns out, there are two components of the market for these devices, a big one and a little one. The big one consists of small businesses, the little one of hobbyists. It is clear that the hobbyist group did not and will not grow into a mass market. Computing will become a mass phenomenon when it enters the American home in the form of an inexpensive, easy-to-operate terminal that is hooked up to a network offering a rich menu of information services ranging from entertainment to educational and training packages. The net result of such a development would be the creation of yet another center of control. There are interesting parallels in this projection with Innis' "monopolies of knowledge".

RESPONSIBILITY AND SOCIAL CONTROL

The reason I have focused on social control is that computer technology has, in its systemic effects, an important influence on the exercise of responsibility by individuals. Moral philosophers since Aristotle have pointed to the indispensability of practice in the exercise of ethical judgment. Ethical judgment is not an inborn capacity; it is a skill that can atrophy from disuse. Any social development that reduces opportunities for exercising significant ethical judgments will inevitably weaken the ability to make such judgments (Mowshowitz, 1978).

A major systemic influence of computer technology is its contribution to fragmentation, reductionism, Taylorism, and the separation of control from task performance. The preservation of the values upon which the best traditions of Western civilization rest requires personal autonomy and opportunity to make principled decisions. The degree to which computers contribute to fragmentation and to limited opportunities for exercising control in the workplace and in the political arena equals the degree to which computers contribute to the erosion of responsible actions. Neither improved security nor education can fully compensate for the lack of organizational settings that allow for and encourage the exercise of significant ethical choice.

REFERENCES

von Gierke, Otto. *Political Theories of the Middle Ages.* Cambridge, England: Cambridge University Press, 1900.

Innis, Harold A. *The Bias of Communication.* Toronto: University of Toronto Press, 1951.

Laudon, Kenneth C. *Computers and Bureaucratic Reform.* New York: John Wiley, 1974.

Mowshowitz, Abbe. "Computers and Ethical Judgment in Organizations." In *ACM 78: Proceedings of the 1978 Annual Conference.* Washington, D.C.: Association for Computing Machinery, 1978.

. . . . "On Approaches to the Study of Social Issues in Computing." *Communications of the ACM 24* (March 1981), 146–155.

Nisbet, Robert. *The Quest for Community.* Oxford, England: Oxford University Press, 1953.

Discussion

Mowshowitz: I think we have focused on complementary problems, looking at some of the immediate questions having to do with human-machine interfaces on the one hand, and long-term systemic effects on the other. I have no particular quarrel with my colleague, except that I prefer my emphasis.

Emery: Well, I will have to comment on that. It seems to me that we reach the long term through the short term, and the way we deal with the problems that we are raising is through successful implementation of systems that meet incremental needs. I don't really see any other alternative to doing that. The question is, can we design systems that can go through a long-term adaptation process of gradual improvement? I think that the methodology exists, if we have the intelligence to use it.

Mowshowitz: Unfortunately, focusing on the problems of implementing user-friendly systems may divert attention from more critical social problems. Consider the intense discussion taking place in Europe these days, in which I think the fate of social democracy hangs in the balance. Europeans are faced with what they see as a real dilemma with regard to the development of microelectronics technology, in both the production of chips and their application. The position of government is this: if it does support the technology, if it invests money in creating production facilities and in encouraging small and medium-sized businesses to incorporate these new devices, it is likely to be faced with increased transfer payments through unemployment. Everyone seems to be convinced of this, that microelectronics will contribute to unemployment. I'm not saying that this is inevitable, but everyone is convinced of it. The reason I say it is a dilemma is that if government does not go ahead and invest money in this new technology and its application, it is going to be faced with the same problem because of the erosion of its competitive position internationally. Some policy initiatives have been taken on the European scene. In fact, most countries are going ahead and investing in various ways, from direct investment in a manufacturing company to making funds available to help small and medium-sized businesses make use of microelectronics in the products they manufacture. But in any case, my point here is that by looking exclusively at the problems of designing and implementing user-friendly systems, one is ignoring, or at the very least minimizing, some real problems that even the best user-friendly systems will generate.

O'Connell: On that basis, let's open up the discussion.

Question: Some of the more astute commentators on totalitarian governments have lamented the tendency of these governments to destroy the mediating structures in a society—that is, those voluntary associations that mediate between the individual and the collective society. This relates to something Mr. Coates tripped off in my mind earlier in his comments. We have, on the one hand, the tendency of the computer to collectivize and amass information; and, on the other, the tendency toward individualization, greater autonomy of the individual, and so forth. And something in that frightens me. I don't think it is enough that the computer can both give us the services for mass information and, at the same time, increase individual autonomy. I was wondering if one of the things you might attempt to suggest as an ethical obligation on our part is the joining and reinforcement of those structures that mediate between the individual and the collective. And I was wondering if you thought there was any way computer technology can help to do this.

Mowshowitz: In a way, your question seems to me to be putting the cart before the horse. I share your concern about the need to reinforce structures that mediate between the individual and the collective. But this need is not unique to dealing with the threat of totalitarian regimes. It is a general consequence of the emergence of the nation state. Intermediate associations have not been eliminated altogether, but they have certainly been weakened in their influence on people's lives. Computer technology appears to contribute to this tendency by supporting centralized bureaucracies. Asking what this technology can do puts the cart before the horse in a different way: a cause of a problem is looked upon as a potential means for its solution. I don't think this is a problem that can be solved by technology. Indeed, focusing on computer applications as a means of solving social problems obscures the origins of those problems and weakens our ability to analyze and resolve them. In the 1970s there were several interesting experiments that attempted to use computers as a means of developing centers of countervailing power within local communities. These experiments were total failures, and as far as I know, they have produced no issue. Basically these experiments were attempts by dissatisfied elements in the computing world—a tiny group of highly skilled programmers, systems analysts, and so forth in several American cities and in Canada—to find a niche for themselves outside of the established corporate world. What they did was to create community memories and information exchanges—computerized data bases containing socially useful information for the average citizen. In one experiment that I know of, several terminals were set up in a public library and anyone could walk in off the street and access the data bases that were made available. There was considerable public interest in this. People did come in, they did use the terminals. But there wasn't enough support—certainly not enough financial support—to continue it. So it just died off. Technological fixes succeed mainly in the fantasies of enthusiasts and promoters of new techniques.

Emery: I think that information technologists have a special burden—for the very reason that we are the custodians of a very powerful technology. If we were to catalog all of our most pressing social problems, I would say that in almost every case a well-designed system can make a contribution. It would be hard to argue that such systems can solve the problems of crime, lack of education, alienation of people in a mass society, and the like, but it seems to me that the problems have at least practical remedies through well-designed systems.

Question: Dr. Emery made a distinction between effectiveness of information technology and efficiency of information technology.

And I think this distinction makes poignant some research done by the Prokoser Research Organization in California on local government, in which it was found that in many cases computing makes government agencies more efficient but does not improve their services to the public. In fact, in some cases it is said to weaken that service. That, in my mind, raises interesting ethical problems because different strategies for implementation of decision making on this issue are not exactly accountable to the public. The public does not normally have any mechanisms to make its sentiments felt on that process one way or another. And I wondered if any of you would care to respond to that.

Emery: I have an immediate response. One of the things it seems to me we ought to get across strongly to the public is that they should not tolerate bad systems. And, in fact, this should be true not just for citizens, but also for workers and managers in organizations. Managers have very poor notions of what they should expect from an information system. They may know that they have bad systems, but they don't know whether their experience is the norm or not, or whether they can do something to improve the situation. All of us should take it as a matter of faith that bad systems should not be accepted as the norm. Good systems can be designed and implemented, using the methodologies that we have now. If we have systems that treat us in insensitive, nonindividualized ways, we ought to know that it is not necessary. We ought to be able to tell the politicians that they cannot take recourse in the argument that in order to be efficient they must treat us as standard pegs. Precisely the opposite is possible. And we ought to get that message across.

Question: I see a great gulf between you. Professor Emery said that if we build a good system, things will move along well; Dr. Mowshowitz was addressing the social context in which the systems are introduced. I would like to see you address this difference: What is "good" and what constitutes a good system?

Emery: I'm willing to concede that we can make incremental improvements and that these improved methodologies and improved systems can at some point be misused by a totalitarian regime, or in a lot of other undesirable ways. In a way, I approach this problem in the same way as I approach it in organizations. MIS people always complain that people are very resistant to change. A more accurate view is that people are resistant to a bad system—one, for example, that cannot tolerate errors. We have a concept called "robustness." A robust system is one that can tolerate errors: it detects errors; it can give guidance by asking, "Do you really mean you have thirty-four children or is that the age of your wife?" to use Joe's illustration. We have friendly systems that are instructive, that guide the user by the hand, perhaps giving different levels of instruction depending on the experience of the user. A friendly system may even be adaptive in that it doesn't instruct you until you get into problems. If you get into problems, it then provides help.

I didn't mean to avoid the moral question of how "good" systems might be misused. But a technically good system, I would argue, is something we should strive for. It may well be that the better the systems are, in a technical sense, the more they then become a tool of suppression on the part of the people who gain control over them. I would not ever argue, however, that the way out of this dilemma is to continue to design bad systems that can't integrate information, cannot be flexible, and cannot serve the needs of their users. That would be similar to the argument that we're better off having an inefficient government because the more efficient the government is, the greater the risk we face of losing our liberties. I don't buy such an argument. I would rather design efficient systems, and operate efficient governments, and deal with their potential abuses as a separate issue. Relying on a crew of incompetent systems designers as a bulwark of our liberties is a risky proposition.

Mowshowitz: I'd like to comment further on that. As a computer scientist I couldn't very well reject the idea of designing good systems, whatever good systems may be. But as an analyst of social phenomena relating to the use of computers, I'd say to you that your point is well taken, that there is a difference here in terms of the implications of good systems, what they are used for ultimately, and what effects they are going to have. I've been talking about long-term systemic effects. And I think that to some extent, even the best systems—in fact, almost all systems, insofar as they do have a bias that they inherit from the social realm in which they are designed and operated—will have certain effects that, in the long run, may not be desirable. And I'm speaking here of the rationalizing bias that the development of computer technology does have. There's no escaping that. One of the consequences of this rationalizing bias is the separation of the control of activity from the activity itself. This has many, many different terms associated with it—Taylorism or reductionism or "de-skilling." We are seeing, I think, contrary to what Joe Coates said earlier, direct effects of the "de-skilling" of clerical workers within the office, and on a large scale.

This is why it is important to make a strong distinction between what a technology is capable of contributing to and supporting in principle, on the one hand, and what, in fact, it achieves or supports, on the other. And if you look at word-processing equipment or other pieces of office automation, you can see the possibility of liberating various jobs that are perhaps dead-end or not very interesting. But in fact, that is not what happens. First of all, note the reasons that employers introduce various pieces of office equipment. The average factory worker in the United States is backed up by something like $25,000 worth of capital equipment; the average office worker is backed up by a mere $2,000 worth. We're talking about productivity increases. You introduce some capital equipment and you get higher productivity in the office. And what this means is that a factory model is applied to the office situation. You get "de-skilling" of clerical workers, and the actuality turns out to be very different from the rather hype-filled predictions of what is possible. And I think that in the long run, this rationalizing bias that contributes to the separation of control from past performance, which is one of the basic contributions of the factory system of production, leads to certain fundamental ethical weaknesses. And this occurs precisely because of what I said before—that the exercise of ethical judgment is a skill, not an inborn capacity; if it is not used, it will atrophy. And it can only be used if people have the opportunity, if they have the autonomy, and if they have the control or the power to make and exercise significant judgments.

Emery: I wonder if I can respond to that. I hesitate to generalize on the basis of a small sample, but my experience in using word processing is apparently quite contrary to yours. When I was president of EDUCOM, we introduced word processing. After a certain period of learning, the system is now totally integrated into the office operations. All securities now have access to a terminal. For the most part, they use it casually, that is, they still spend no more of their time typing than they did before. Most of them have not become specialists in word processing. I have the strong feeling that they greatly appreciate having that capability. It makes their job much easier. We also see some of the professional staff using the word processing system directly, because it is a friendly, easy-to-use system that reduces the level of typing skill one needs to use it productively. I think one of the things we're learning is that this approach is the best way to introduce office automation—that is, with relatively little disruption of office routine and based on voluntary use.

I don't know whether this example refutes your point, that the technology is a threat to employment. In organizations that I have observed, the secretarial staff generally perceives office automation as being in their interests. In general, it has not resulted in what one could measure as a productivity gain, such as a reduction in employment. What happens is that style of working tends to change. People now prepare half a dozen drafts of a technical document, whereas before they did everything they could to reduce the number of times they had to retype the document. Most organizations that have looked seriously at office automation understand that the goal is to improve the productivity and effectiveness of the professional and managerial staffs, not reduce the employment level of secretaries.

O'Connell: Can I back off just a minute, lest we lose one of the themes we will need for the balance of the conference? To narrate, at some risk, a personal experience, seven years ago this week I was in a group facing a white-coated computer specialist in what almost appeared to be an operating theater. Through the glass in the background, lights were blinking on from what I hoped were robust and friendly bits of equipment. The presentation was one that appeared to be rather optimistic in terms of political science and political philosophy. The speaker was describing how this technology would very soon permit true democracy in that you would have a red and a green button at home, and through this communication device we could really have a populist democracy voting through a national referendum on all issues. That room was in the Cybernetics Institute in Kiev. I wonder if the speaker earlier did not go far enough in terms of building friendly and robust systems. The question is, for what?

Question: I'm very interested in the design of knives-for-mad-people illustration. As a noncomputer person, I'd like to know how much resistance there is in the industry and among the scientists themselves to designing advanced computer technology for both the mad allies we have, and also for the part of our own lives that participates in madness. Just how much turmoil is there in the discussion about the manufacture of sophisticated handguns and the distributing of them?

Mowshowitz: I'll take a stab at that. In my experience as a teacher and as a consultant, I would say that there is a very little turmoil or concern within the industry among computer scientists generally about the impact of computer technology or the kinds of projects that they actually work on. I think it is accurate to generalize from my experiences as a teacher, having introduced a course in a computer science department on the social impact of computing. Even with a captive audience and after a whole semester of control over the environment, I think that it really made very little impression on computer science students who were about to go out and join the work force. There are much more immediate questions that concern them, both of a technical nature and of a personal nature. And these somewhat diffuse and difficult to verify impacts simply leave them cold.

I recently had some dealings with the maritime industry, and one interesting contrast came out. If a steamship company introduces an automated crane, that's a huge visible piece of equipment which they drag next to the pier for loading and unloading containers. On the other hand, if they introduce a computer or a terminal someplace, it is a very subtle intrusion in the workspace. This question arose because the maritime union on the West Coast has a clause in their contract that involves technical change. They're supposed to have advance notice of any kind of technical change. Now if the company is going to introduce a new crane, there's no question that they're going to have to give the union advance notice. Yet if they put a video display terminal on the dock somewhere, for use by a marine clerk, it's rather questionable what's going on and what impact the change has. Computer technology is much more subtle and its implications are more difficult to trace.

O'Connell: Just one bit of evidence from outside our own country, in response. Many of you know about the participation schemes in the Scandinavian countries, the Lowlands and Germany. In the TCO, for instance, which is the white collar union in Sweden, the activist group in the union consists of the computer science people. Their employers would refer to them as the overeducated and underbusy, and therefore politically active. But there is no doubt that employers associations across Europe would identify the leaders of employee activist groups as members of the information systems field.

Comment: Could I comment briefly on the indifference of computer technologists? I think electrical engineering of computers in the United States is a mass professional occupation, and the people who have moved into it in the last fifteen years are essentially lower middle class and working class in their origin. What they bring to their new professionalism is a peculiar sense of loyalty—loyalty to the dollar, loyalty to their employer. I think this is fundamentally a class problem: the people who will become the new professionals have no sense of autonomy, independence, social responsibility. And that can be a potential disaster.

Mowshowitz: I wonder if any class has ever had a monopoly on social responsibility.

Comment: Well, let me give you an example. The professional group in the United States that has been most socially responsible since World War II has been the physicists. And the origin of American physicists is largely upper middle-class, professional, managerial—people from the top of the heap who are educated from age zero in social responsibility.

O'Connell: To the intellectual, America's unforgivable sin is that it has revolutions without revolutionaries, and achieves the momentous in a very matter-of-fact, prosaic way. Wouldn't it be fun to have a revolutionary we could shoot at?

CHAPTER 3

Ethical Dilemmas in Computer Technology

*Donn B. Parker**

In discussing the ethical implications of computer technology, we have been putting the cart before the horse. We should get a consensus on the application of ethics to the computer field *before* we start writing our codes of ethics, rather than after. There isn't much of a consensus yet, but that ought to be a reasonable place to start to determine the applications of ethics to this new technology.

This need for a consensus was the basis for a study conducted at the Stanford Research Institute (SRI) in 1977 where we assembled about thirty-five people together for three days. It was started as a highly scientific experiment in which experimenting with methodology was part of the study. However, that deteriorated rather rapidly when we decided to try for richer results by forgoing the scientific aspects and using instead a scenario technique that hadn't been used previously, at least in this way.

We wrote about sixty half-page scenarios about individuals who are in trouble of some kind or have to make some kind of personal ethical decision concerning some aspect of the computer field.

We produced some simple, neutral-variant scenarios and sent them to participants in advance. We said, here is a little story; tell us about the ethics of the individual who made a decision in this little story, and vote on whether that individual was not unethical,

*Senior Management Systems Consultant, Stanford Research Institute International

unethical, or whether there was an ethical issue at all. We had them give us their opinions about these stories and identify any of the underlying principles. We asked them to vote, but not on exemplary ethical activity. We were trying to distinguish between what is unethical and what is not unethical.

We then brought them together for three days in confrontations in small groups and large groups to argue out some of the opinions and principles concerning the scenarios. They produced another forty scenarios and we ended up with a total of almost a hundred. It was very much an empirical process. Several lawyers in the group tried to keep us from getting too far into legal issues, and several ethical philosophers tried to keep us from getting bogged down in deep philosophical issues that some of the rest of us did not understand. We had an interesting combination of technologists, managers, ethical philosophers, and lawyers, and it all worked well.

Then we empirically classified the scenarios by topics. We created the scenarios first, mostly based on the hundreds of cases of reported computer abuses in the SRI files, and then categorized them in various ways. There were seven categories. The first concerned conflict over obligations having to do with unauthorized use of computers, such as for game playing or for church mailing lists or bowling scores or for other personal purposes; it also included attacking and trying to crash computers as a game. The second issue was disputed rights to products, including the property rights to computer programs and data and the copying of such kinds of intellectual property assets. The third issue concerned the confidentiality of data having to do mostly with the privacy issue, emphasizing decisions that computer programmers or computer operators must make when confronted with a position of trust in protecting, or having to do with the confidentiality of personal information stored in computers with which they are involved.

The fourth topic concerned conflicts in personal morality having to do with professional ethics and organizational loyalty. An example is the reporting of suspected fraud involving the use of computers and the harm that might be done from ill-defined or partially implemented systems—some of the things that Jim Emery spoke about, including reporting incompetence or refusing to accept incompetence when there are lives or people's private activities at stake. The fifth issue involved the responsibility of the social effects of computer applications, such as displacing workers through automation. The last issue focused on responsibility for influencing public opinion, including the use of computers as tools for deception or intimidation.

Arthur Miller had a fascinating experience when he was defending a doctor in Michigan. The prosecutor came into the courtroom with a huge stack of computer listings and was going to show how the computer proved that the doctor had acted fraudulently, and it was the computer that was going to prove this. In another incident a little company in Texas sent invoices out to people. That was their entire business; they just sent invoices to people all over the country. It turns out that a lot of people were willing to pay bills. It was a very low overhead operation, and although they did have a lot of complaints, they took care of them very nicely by sending a form letter that said, "We're sorry we sent this invoice to you by mistake. Our computer made an error." Of course, anybody will believe anything you tell them if you tell them a computer made an error.

Those are the kind of problems we dealt with. The validity of computer tools in decision making and our reliance on automated decision making and the kinds of unethical things that could be done were described in half-page scenarios. Some of the ethical issues that we considered were: when does a program belong to the programmer who wrote it and when does it belong to his employer who paid for it? Should idle computers be used for personal purposes on an unauthorized basis? A lot of people in the field feel that this is acceptable behavior.

Three years ago I polarized the academic community by making a statement that was quoted in the press in which I said that we are creating a new generation of computer criminals in our computer science departments. My position was based on the fact that the application of ethics had never been introduced into computer science departments. Some faculty members said they don't deal with ethics, only with computers.

Business schools, medical schools, and engineering schools in varying degrees pass ethical principles from professor to student either formally or informally. In computer science departments I found some very thoughtful computer science professors who *do* impart ethical concerns to their students but many more who never even bother to think about the subject and in fact, do the opposite because they encourage their students to attack the university computer systems as a game and as a means of learning how these systems operate. Now there is certainly a place for doing that in an academic community to determine weaknesses in computer systems. But when you throw out the challenge to an entire university and say, in effect, come and attack our system, or when you encourage the development of computer crash clubs where someone can join the crash club if he has proven that he has crashed the university's computer system without detection, then I think we have a lot of problems.

When I voiced these concerns about three years ago, it created quite a controversy, but ever since then it has been very interesting that some universities have been criminally prosecuting their students for doing these kinds of things. Joe Coates mentioned the Dalton School case. We've recently been investigating some of these cases. At the University of Alberta three teenagers, one of them addicted to computers, were convicted. One of the convictions was later overturned because of a shortcoming in the law. At DePaul University, a sixteen year old and a seventeen year old caused $22,000 worth of damage in DePaul University's computer system. At the University of California at Berkeley the Concord whiz kid caused many thousands of dollars worth of damage.

Serious problems have occurred at Georgia Tech and Queens College where the students were charging a fee for changing grades and had elevated themselves into the Phi Beta Kappa. Similar occurrences can be cited at the University of Wisconsin, Dartmouth, Cal Tech, Washington University, University of Michigan; in fact, every university I have visited has a serious and growing problem of high school students and university and college students compromising computer systems and causing problems.

Part of the faculty is saying they're just kids, that's just games, they're learning a tremendous amount by doing that, it's an innocuous activity. The other side is saying, these kids that are learning to compromise computers here are going out to work in banks and they're carrying the concept of game playing with them, and you don't play games in vaults! It's just not acceptable to do that; these kids ought to learn this in school before they are thrust out into very high positions of trust without ever having encountered ethical applications in their work in universities.

In any case, let me go on and consider the positions that programmers are thrust into, such as those in which they are actually the ones who are determining the algorithms by which banks charge interest. Bank management thinks it knows what its computer is doing, but there are hundreds of ways to calculate interest. It is only the programmer who really knows what is in that computer program, and hopefully, he has followed the directions of management. But no one really knows for sure because people don't normally read the programs of others. We are trying to change that with structured programming techniques, but it still represents a problem.

Our goal was not to create new principles or to get a consensus on principles but simply to introduce the idea that maybe we ought to have a few written down on a piece of paper. For example, there are two principles that we might consider regarding proprietariness of computer programs. Should we in computer technology consider a computer program always to be in the public domain unless it is explicitly identified as being proprietary? This is consistent with the law, but I objected to that principle as a basis for ethics because it gets people into trouble far too easily. I think we should use the far more cautious concept that we should always treat a computer program as though it belongs to somebody unless it is explicitly identified to be in the public domain. This is far more cautious and, I think, the more professional ethical approach to this particular issue. Others, however, argue strongly that this is ridiculous.

The former principle leads to an ethic derived from the following incident. A well-known consultant on a witness stand in a computer crime trial told the judge that it is his practice that as long as you are paying for the computer time, anything you can find in a time-shared computer system is automatically in the public domain, and you can do with it as you please unless it is explicitly identified to be proprietary. The judge was astounded at this and asked if that was an industry principle. The witness had to admit that it was his own value and the value of his associates.

This issue has led to all kinds of problems where people fish around in other people's computers trying to find things and then use them or obtain them, assuming that they are in the public domain because they could obtain them through whatever means. This is almost like saying that anything in a store is available for the taking unless printed on it is the statement, "This Is the Property of" followed by the name of the official owner. There is an implied indication of ownership on an item on a store counter; the status of such an item is governed by property and purchase rights and obligations, infringement of which is subject to legal action. But when it comes to computer programs residing in computers, these principles have never really been worked out.

It is a difficult issue, and there is a lot of disagreement on it, as I will now demonstrate. I want to use my audience here for a little experiment and give you an idea of what we went through in considering ethical issues. I'm going to tell you a story, and I'm going to ask you to vote whether you think the actor in the scenario was unethical or not unethical.

Now, what do I mean by scenario? Well you may remember the owner of an appliance store whose son asked him one day, "Dad, what is ethics?" The father replied, "Well, son, let me give you a little scenario to demonstrate what is ethics. A woman came into my store and bought a refrigerator, and she paid $100 too much for it. She left the store before I realized that she had overpaid. Now, son, ethics is the issue, should I tell my partner about it?" Was the owner of this appliance store unethical in what he was about to do or was he not unethical?

For many of the scenarios, we got a preponderance of people who said, "That's clearly unethical or yes, that's very clearly not unethical," but what really disturbed us all as we sat there voting is that many of these scenarios seemed as though they were simple, and yet all of a sudden someone would say, "That's unethical" and someone with equally valid reasons would say, "That is not unethical, that's perfectly reasonable to do." We got a lot of very close votes. In other words, we were not able to obtain consensus on what is unethical or not unethical in the computer field.

So, let me give you a little scenario: I will tell you this story and I'll let you ask me some questions about the story; then I'll ask you to vote on whether you thought the person in the story was unethical or not unethical in what he did. The scenario concerns a programmer, his employer, his new employer, and a valuable computer program. This computer programmer wrote an application program for his employer, and his employer paid him to do it the way an employer normally pays an employee to write a computer program. The programmer quit his job, having accepted a job with a competitor of his employer. In cleaning out his desk, he picked up a copy of the computer program, leaving the original, took the copy with him to his new employer, and offered it to his new employer for his use. The question is, was this programmer unethical in doing that or was he not unethical in doing that?

Question: What was the contractual relationship of the programmer?

Parker: It was a normal contractual relationship between employee and employer.

Question: Verbal?

Parker: He did not sign any papers other than the usual patent agreement.

Question: What kind of industry was it? Was it the United States government? Did he go to work for Russia?

Parker: I'll only say that this took place in businesses that are competing. And so it could have been the financial industry, the chemical industry, or whatever.

The approximate vote in our group was: unethical, 94; not un-ethical, 16.

From this vote, we get a limited consensus that a programmer should discuss this with his employer before running off with the program. In our study at SRI, twenty-seven people voted; twenty-six said this was unethical and one said it was not unethical. You can see that this audience had a different split.

The next scenario is a variation, involving a programmer, an employer, a new employer, and a personal program. A program-mer wrote a utility program. He did not tell his employer about it. He wrote it for his own personal use, using his employer's resources and time. He used it to make himself more productive for his em-ployer. He left his employer, went to work for a competitor, took all copies of the program with him, and used the program to increase his productivity with the new employer.

Question: How much of the first employer's resources and time in the computer did he use? Did he use it during his lunch break or did he take several hours a day with it?

Parker: I'll answer that by saying that he used a significant amount of his employer's regular working time, computer time, to develop the program.

Question: Did the increased productivity that he derived from that development make up for the use of the employer's resources?

Parker: Oh, very much so.

Question: Is there any reason to think that his old employer could have used it, had he just left it?

Parker: Well, only to the extent that anybody could use anybody else's personal program.

Question: But it wasn't developed with that kind of transportabil-ity in mind?

Parker: No, it was not. It was a personal tool.

Question: Was there any kind of promise keeping in person, or otherwise?

Parker: No, nothing.

Question: Did he have the intention of changing jobs when he was developing the program?

Parker: Oh, we can't tell that. I couldn't see inside the man's head to know whether he did that or not. I'll have to leave that for you.

The approximate vote was: unethical, 16; not unethical, 96.

In wrestling with this problem the experts in our workshop arrived at almost a fifty-fifty split. Half of them said it was unethical and the other half said it was not unethical.

These scenarios were taken from a book called *Ethical Conflicts in Computer Science and Technology*. The book contains forty-seven ethical scenarios, all with the opinions and principles ordered by the way a group of experts voted on them. I think you'd find it interesting. And it is set up also for educational purposes with a workbook. The workbook contains only the scenarios and forms for students to fill out with their own opinions and vote, and then compare with what the thirty-five experts did.

The idea of this project was to get the computer scientist, the lawyer, and the ethical pholosopher together to consider these ethical issues with their different areas of expertise. Computer technology is changing the nature of business crime as well as the nature of the application and the circumstances of ethical principles. They're the same old principles by name: fraud, theft, larceny, and embezzlement.

What has been demonstrated here by my report of the SRI workshop results and by your votes is the fact that we have a long way to go. How can we tell students what is right and what is wrong in this new technology if we don't have some kind of agreement among ourselves? Everybody knows the ethical principles. It is their application to technology that we must have some kind of consensus on before we can write codes of ethics.

CHAPTER 4

Ethics Education
in the Field of
Computer Technology

Chapter 4A

Educating Toward
Ethical Responsibility

*Deborah G. Johnson**

There is no doubt that computer technology has had and will continue to have a significant impact on the way we live. Because the effects of extensive computerization threaten some values and support others, questions about the management of computer technology are important. Choices in how we use computer technology have an effect on what we value.

I want to talk briefly about how educational institutions are doing in terms of educating students about the impacts of computers, and then I want to discuss my experiences in undertaking a project on computer ethics at Rensselaer Polytechnic Institute. I do this in the hope of promoting the process of "educating toward ethical responsibility" for computer impacts.

In terms of how educational institutions are doing at present, the answer is simply "not well." I am referring to undergraduate education. More could be said about educating the public and educating professionals who are already working with computers, but when it comes to undergraduate education, we just are not doing very much. If one looks in the EVIST Resource Directory (a directory of courses and programs on ethics and values in science and

*Department of Philosophy and Center for the Study of the Human Dimensions of Science and Technology, Rensselaer Polytechnic Institute

technology) one finds only twenty-two courses listed under the topic "Computers." This is extremely distressing considering the widespread and rapidly expanding use of computers in our society. The reasons for this are hard to pin down and are no doubt complex, but interdisciplinary programs and courses do not usually fare well in our educational system.

Nevertheless I do see some signs of hope, in particular in my own discipline, philosophy. In recent years philosophers have been turning their attention to what they call "applied philosophy" or "applied ethics." The oldest and most developed area in biomedical ethics, but more recently philosophers have been looking at business ethics, engineering ethics, and ethics and public policy. Several philosophy departments have also begun to teach courses (not listed in the EVIST directory) on Computer Ethics. For example, Walter Maner at Old Dominion University has taught a course on Computer Ethics for at least two years now. John Snapper at IIT instituted a new course this past year entitled "Moral Issues in Computer Science." In the hope of furthering this movement, I want to share my experience in developing materials and a course at Rensselaer.

We received a small grant from the Local Course Improvement program of the National Science Foundation (NSF) to develop (1) materials that could be incorporated into a Computing Fundamentals course and (2) a full semester course on Social-Ethical Issues in Computing. Our project built on the work Donn Parker had done in his EVIST project, "Ethical Conflicts in Computer Science and Technology." For that project a number of scenarios had been developed. The scenarios involved individuals working with computers and presented situations that might require an ethical decision.

During the first phase of our project we did a bibliographic search and met regularly with computer science faculty to talk about the modules we were to develop. We then developed three modules using Parker's scenarios but developing a more theoretical discussion of them. We tested these modules by presenting them at different points in various Computing Fundamentals sections and in different sequences. Based on feedback, we redesigned the modules and retested them in a subsequent semester. Once we had the modules fairly well designed, we began to plan and design the full semester course, which was offered in spring of 1980. This is a very brief summary of what we did. The details will come out as I discuss different aspects of our experience.

RATIONALE

Part of the rationale for undertaking this project we knew in advance and part of it we discovered along the way. We began with the idea that making people aware of the ethical issues related and associated with computing was a necessary, even if not a sufficient, condition for getting them to behave ethically. We knew, that is, that in order for people to behave ethically they have to be aware that there is a problem or an issue. This seems particularly important in the case of computers because some of the issues, while not complex, are not obvious because of the new context. The best example of this is the lack of concern that many people have about using a computer account that is not theirs. For some reason this is not always perceived as stealing, which is what it is. Thus one may believe in a certain ethical principle but then not see that the principle applies in a new context. We wanted, then, simply to make people more aware, make them more sensitive to the kind of subtle issues that might exist when they use computers.

The other rationale for our project had to do with a new approach to computer issues. We were aware that research and courses had already been developed on the social impacts of computing but these questions had seldom been addressed in terms of professional ethics. Not many people had focused on the idea that computer professionals were faced with decisions that had an ethical component. And so even though a student might have a course on the social impacts of computing, that course wouldn't necessarily address the question, "What does that mean to me as a professional?" "It is true," students might say, "that computers have an impact, but what can I do about it?" What was needed, then, was a course and materials that would take the social impact research and focus it in a way that would be useful to future computer professionals. Donn Parker's scenarios were well suited for this approach. Our emphasis, then, was to make students aware of the ethical issues surrounding computers by focusing the issues around scenarios that raised questions about what people working with computers ought to do.

POSITIVE RESULTS

Some very good things occurred and are still occurring as a result of our teaching modules, but we encountered a number of problems along the way. First of all, one of the things that we were very pleased with was that the Computer Science faculty was very receptive and very responsive. After we had presented the modules and then tested them, redesigned them, and tested them again, the Computer Science Department had done all that it had promised. Although we had not gotten their permission to make the modules a permanent part of the course, we were called back each semester to come in and present the materials, and the modules have informally become a regular part of some sections of the Computing Fundamentals course. In fact, when it was not possible for us to teach the sections, the Computer Science faculty took over and presented the materials themselves. One very positive result was that the Computer Science faculty liked the idea, encouraged us, and approved of what we were doing.

Furthermore, the student response was encouraging. In general the students reported that the module materials did make them more aware of ethical issues. They said that the modules made them aware of things that they had not been aware of before and helped them to work through the ethical problems a little bit more than they would have been able to without the materials.

Even more important than these two results was the fact that the subject matter turned out to be extremely rich in terms of showing us that there were in fact a number of rather serious ethical issues. Not being computer professionals ourselves, we were not sure that we could find enough to keep us busy or enough material to enable us to show that in fact computer professionals can do something about social impact issues. But it turned out that many of the students who had jobs would bring in examples of issues we had not thought of, or could refer to situations where they would in fact be in a position to affect the ethical implications of what they were doing. For example, they would point out that a system could be designed in more than one way and if it were designed in one way rather than another, the possibility of abuse could be avoided.

Earlier Donn Parker drew a distinction regarding the need for a policy when we do not know whether information stored on a computer is in the public domain or not. We could assume that it is in the public domain unless it is explicitly identified as not being in the public domain, *or* we could assume that it is not in the public domain unless it is explicitly identified as such. This is a good example of how the approach that you take can affect behavior and also is an example of how someone who works with computers can make a difference. If computer professionals are aware of this distinction they can make a choice, but if they simply make one of those assumptions without being aware of the alternative, then their behavior is blind.

The most encouraging aspects of our undertaking were therefore faculty response, student response, and the richness of the material.

PROBLEMS AND ISSUES

Let us look now at some of the problems that have to be faced in educating toward ethical responsibility, beginning with student response. The response in general to our materials was positive, but as you can probably guess we found that the students (at least a large portion of them) were very skeptical. They are skeptical in the sense that they think all discussion of ethics is just "talk" and when it gets right down to it, you do what your boss tells you or you do what will secure your job. If you describe situations where a person's self-interest conflicts with a moral principle, they see only that you are trying to convince them that they ought to abide by the moral principle, but they believe that really we all will act from self-interest, and that a person would be foolish not to.

This is a problem not unique to teaching computer science students; it is a problem in any kind of course on ethics. It struck me as one of the hardest things to deal with in terms of material, because we do not want to be perceived as handing down doctrine; we want students to discuss the material within an openended framework so that they will develop their analytical skills. But we also do not want them to think that there are no answers, no right and wrong. So the fact that students are going to be skeptical (both about ethics in general and about this whole process of teaching ethics) is something that has to be attended to carefully in courses on computer ethics.

In terms of the students another issue that was a partial problem, but I think not a serious one, was that in general if the students are primarily computer science majors, then they are attuned to a certain kind of technical material and a certain kind of classroom structure. This is particularly so at RPI, an engineering school. Students are accustomed to courses in which questions are asked for which the answers are very straightforward: the teacher gives information and then asks for it back on tests. Students are therefore most comfortable with technical problems that have fairly well-defined answers; they are not comfortable with openended kinds of settings and openended problems. Also because they tend to be rather taken by technology, they tend to think that every problem can be solved by technology. If you present them with an ethical issue that arises as a result of computers or situations associated with computing, their immediate reaction is to say—"Look, there is a technological solution to this; we can just design computers this way, or set up the computers in a different way." The students therefore tend to make the mistake that Abbe Mowshowitz pointed out: they tend to think that technology has the potential to be used in many different ways; thus talking about computers and their effects doesn't make a lot of sense. This means that they have to be confronted with discussions of social and political issues and shown how the social-political context means that computers *will* be used in one way rather than another. Because these students tend to see technological solutions to problems, I tend to keep trying to push them to see that issues exist that cannot be solved by technology, that is, that deeper social-political issues must be addressed.

Now let us turn to another sort of problem. Who should teach or offer such courses? How should they be taught? One of the realities we must face is that in an academic setting, there are no incentives to do this sort of course. In fact there are disincentives. Courses on computer ethics and on the impact of computers are interdisciplinary. You have to know something about computing and you have to know something about ethics. If you are a philosopher, then your disciplinary colleagues may look down on you for doing something that has to do with computing (you are supposed to be doing "philosophy"). And if you are in computer science you may get very little credit for what you do in terms of the social impacts; social impact courses may not be recognized as legitimate because they are not pure computer science. So very often the people who take these kinds of courses do them as an overload; they don't take them for credit, and they are not recognized as something important in terms of their professional lives.

In our experience, at least in teaching the modules, we concluded that it was really important that this material should *not* be presented as extraneous to the technical information. The ethical and social issues should be combined with the technical material. On the other hand, the reality is that instructors are under pressure in introductory computer science courses to cover a lot of material. At RPI they were willing to give us a week, but they really couldn't give us much more, and I think our feeling was that a week just wasn't enough. It was enough to get people interested a little bit and get them stimulated, but not really to do anything very serious and rigorous. Nevertheless we thought that a week-long module *integrated* in the course was better than only presenting the material separately in another course.

The full semester course became important as a follow-up to the modules. If students got interested from the modules, they could and would, we believed, pursue their interests further in a regular course. So we developed one. The first problem we encountered was that there really is not a lot of material. To be sure, there is plenty of material on the social impacts of computers, but what we wanted was material that would focus on professional ethical issues. We found that when presented with descriptive materials on the social impacts of computers, the students find it interesting but it does not get to them. Using Parker's scenarios was most successful because the scenarios confront the students with something they can identify with. They are forced to ask what their responsibility will be as a professional and how they will handle, for example, a conflict between professional duty and conscience. Still the Parker materials do not provide an indepth analysis of the issues. Our problem therefore was to take social impact materials and Parker's scenarios and work them up into a rich, integrated whole. In other words these materials do not have the ethical concepts needed to present the material from a professional ethical point of view. We did this work-up primarily in class discussion, but much more needs to be done to develop materials for these courses.

Who should teach such courses? Should it be a philosopher? Should it be a computer scientist? Given what I said earlier about the ethical issues being posed alongside the technical material, it seems that, ideally, these courses should be team-taught. But as I said before, the institutional incentives do not seem to make this likely. In fact, the reality is that in computer science departments, very often there is a shortage of teaching manpower and they cannot afford to teach this kind of a course. Frankly, I don't believe that *expertise* in computer science is essential because the issues are fundamentally ethical and social. Thus a humanist or social scientist who is willing to learn something about computers is capable of developing and teaching such a course.

What sort of content is needed? Our experience suggests at least three types of materials. First, some sort of background in ethical theory, special concepts in ethics in particular, should be presented. The notions that need to be stressed are: (1) Responsibility: What does it mean to be responsible for something? How should we decide who is responsible? (2) Property: How does something become defined as property? What rules govern how one comes to own something? Ownership is not just a natural given. Property is a notion defined by rules—rules that have in fact a moral basis; and those rules define when something becomes yours and how you can transfer it to somebody else. (3) Privacy: People tend to think that it is obvious that privacy is a good thing, but the questions of what privacy is, why it is important, and why people value it all need to be raised. (4) Autonomy: The notion of an individual being in control of his or her self or (being self-determined, being able to control his/her life) needs to be explored. This is important both because of the threat that computers have been said to pose to autonomy and also because it seems that as information is gathered and decision making is centralized it is possible that we are losing control over how our lives are run.

The second component necessary in courses on computer ethics is analysis of the social impacts of computers, both in terms of the kind of impact computers have had and their potential impact. We did this in part by taking computers in certain contexts and looking at how they have already changed particular fields and how they are likely to effect changes in the future, with computers in medicine, computers in business, computers in criminal justice, and computers in education as cases in point. Also in this regard it is useful to present a history of computing that emphasizes why computers have developed at the rate they have, and where and how they have been used.

The third component should address the question of individual responsibility and what individuals can do to formulate public policy and to control the kind of impact that computers have in various sectors. In this component the emphasis is on professional ethics and public policy. This is where we used scenarios.

Teaching courses on computer ethics may not be a sufficient condition for getting people to act ethically, but it is at least a necessary condition that they be aware of the problems, and that is what courses on computer ethics can do. Let me end by saying that it seems to me that the really fundamental question is the question of responsibility. It is an old question, not unique to computer professionals: are individuals responsible for the consequences of what they do? I believe the answer is clearly, yes. On the one hand, if we are made aware of the issues we cannot use ignorance as an excuse. On the other hand, ignorance cannot be an excuse in any case because an individual has some responsibility to think about the consequences of an action before acting. Thus individuals who are working and will work with computers have some responsibility to think about the impact of their work.

Educating Toward Ethical Responsibility in the Teaching of Management Information Systems

*Jeffrey A. Meldman**

I will be talking about a teaching environment that is some-what different from the one that Deborah Johnson described. I teach in a school of management, and I would like to be able to say that we have a strong and comprehensive teaching program in the area of business ethics. We do have a few courses related to corporate responsibility and values, but not all of our students take them. In the area of management information systems we have an even less systematic way of injecting ethical issues into the curriculum. It depends a great deal—and I expect this is true in many other schools as well—on the individual faculty member as to whether, and how, the ethical issues are to be faced. We teach nine MIS courses, ranging from information technology to managerial and legal problems. This provides us with considerable opportunity to find places where ethical issues ought to be addressed. We do this in different ways and I would like to tell you about some of them, although none of these is as elaborate as the project that Deborah Johnson has told us about.

First of all, let me mention our faculty's strong belief that computer literacy is a very necessary component of management education. This is not an unusual point of view; most schools of man-

*M.I.T. Sloan School of Management

agement probably agree with it. But to some extent, this itself helps with some of the kinds of problems we have been discussing today. The more literate managers are about computers—that is, the more they really understand what computers do and the less they have to depend on some of the hocum that others might spout about them—the better they are able to avoid one particular problem that we have identified today: ignorance in action. Many of the problems that we have been talking about stem from the fact that the people in charge do not really understand what it is that they are in charge of. Of course many other problems are associated with people who are using a computer very intelligently for an unethical purpose. Nonetheless we believe that computer literacy is helpful in allowing managers at least to understand what it is they are doing with their computers—as users, as managers, or even as data subjects.

Secondly, we will often inject the question of ethical behavior into discussions of various cases in the information systems area. In doing this, we are perhaps following what Donn Parker earlier called the "microethics" approach: we look at the situation presented and at the ethical issues involved, but we usually do not try to generalize or to formulate basic ethical principles.

A similar method that I have employed in an introductory course in programming and system concepts is to use some of Donn Parker's scenarios in class. I usually devote one out of approximately twenty class periods to this exercise, so we only have time to talk about four or five scenarios. Loosely following the technique of the original study, the class votes after reading each scenario and then votes again after discussing the issues. It is very interesting to see the process by which some students will change their minds as they talk through the issues and the undisclosed assumptions. Our votes are often similar to the votes of the original panel, but I do not really think that these results mean much to the students. It is the discussion itself that I think is important. Donn Parker asked how we can teach what is ethical if we do not understand our own consensus of what is ethical or unethical. I guess I would have to reply that I do not really try to teach what is ethical so much as I try to make the students aware of ethical issues and to take them seriously. Later, when they are faced with similar situations, perhaps they will at least be more likely to recognize and face these issues.

Another vehicle we have used is the TV film, *The Billion Dollar Bubble*. Some of you may be familiar with it. It is a dramatization of certain computer-related aspects of the "Equity Funding scandal" of several years ago. I believe it was broadcast once on one of the networks and it is now distributed by Time-Life Films. I do not mean to make this sound like a commercial for the film, but I must tell you that our faculty and students alike have found the film extraordinarily entertaining while simultaneously exploring some critically important ethical issues rarely discussed in school. The film focuses on the way middle and operational managers can be pressured into going along with questionable company practices and is highly successful in presenting the different kinds of pressures and motivations experienced by different people in different ways: company loyalty, peer pressure, intimidation, technological challenge, and, of course, just plain greed. Often the pressure is subtle and, as is often true in white-collar crime, the initial discomforts are slowly covered over by rationalizations that sound very much like principles of sound management. I believe it is important that our students have more opportunities to be exposed to, and to be able to discuss, pressures and behavior of this kind.

There is another form in which education toward ethical thinking takes place in our courses. I am not a philosopher of ethics and I do not know the correct term for this, but I think of it as the pragmatic approach to ethics—an enlightened utilitarianism. Very often we can demonstrate that it is in our own self-interest, an aspect of the "good system" that James Emery talked about (see Chapter 2A), to do something that might also be considered ethical. Let me give you some examples that are incorporated in our teaching and probably in your teaching as well.

One of the points Emery mentioned, one that has become a cornerstone of good system design, is user involvement. Many of the early failures of information systems in organizations (and many current failures as well) occurred because the future users of the systems were ignored when the system was designed. As a result, these systems were often difficult to use, they made new demands on the user, or they created undesirable organizational or political changes. Users were not motivated to use the system in the manner contemplated by the designer (sometimes they were even motivated to misuse it purposely), and so the systems frequently had to be abandoned. This situation has an ethical thrust as well as a pragmatic thrust, and they both point in the same direction. We might question the ethics of building a system that has negative effects on the users. At the same time we can demonstrate that systems that serve the needs of the user, as well as the needs of the organization, tend to be more successful and more valuable to the organization. Wherever these happy coincidences of ethics and utilitarianism occur, they allow us to piggyback ethical concerns on the shoulders of enlightened self-interest.

Another example that has come up in my classes involves the information systems consultant. Consultants are often brought into an organization midway in the design or implementation process for a new information system. Sometimes it is clear to the consultant at the outset that the system is headed for trouble. He or she has apparently been brought in to rubber-stamp somebody's poor ideas, to rationalize them, to set up a defense, perhaps, against future fault finding. We have cases where this is exactly what seems to be happening. I usually ask my class whether they consider the consultants' behavior to be ethical. What typically happens is that the discussion immediately takes a pragmatic turn. The students tend to express concern over the consultant's reputation: "If he does this too often, he will be associated with a lot of failures," and so forth. This often gives us a chance to discuss the relationship between ethics and practical considerations.

A third example involves the protection of privacy. Very often this issue affects people outside an organization (for example, customers) as well as those within it. Once again, there are pragmatic as well as ethical reasons for trying to protect the personal privacy of data subjects, although until recently not many business organizations seemed to realize this. I believe the first nationwide advertising campaign that pushed privacy as a selling point was the Aetna Insurance campaign of a few years ago. IBM has also run ads that support the protection of privacy. But it has been only recently that privacy has been considered as something that might be used to sell products and services, and I do not know whether it has been successful. I have discovered that the most forceful way to promote the protection of privacy is to discuss legal requirements and potential liabilities. I find that students—particularly practicing managers who are taking continuing education courses—are not as interested in the ethics of privacy as they are in avoiding the costly litigation that is possible under the increasing volume of privacy laws. I have mixed feelings about piggybacking an ethical issue onto a pragmatic threat, but I try to include both aspects. The pragmatic approach certainly sells better.

This example also raises the issue of the relationship between legal requirements and liabilities, on the one hand, and ethical responsibility, on the other. I teach a course in information systems and law in which we constantly face the question of whether or not legal restrictions should be viewed as the boundaries of ethical behavior. I think it is unfortunate that we sometimes teach law in business schools as a kind of substitute for ethics. It is true of course that the law to some extent embodies and teaches the ethical norms of society. At the same time, this approach leads some people in the business world to believe that there is nothing left to ethical behavior beyond what is required by law. You will often find business organizations such as those discussed here taking the attitude, "We're not doing anything unethical because what we're doing is perfectly legal." Whether or not we want to leave the impression with our students that law is a perfectly acceptable surrogate for ethics is something that ought to be examined more carefully.

Finally, I would like to suggest that in our striving to educate toward ethical business behavior, the universities must necessarily share responsibility with business organizations themselves. We all know that a lot of education takes place on the job, and this is particularly true with respect to role models and the pressure to follow organizational norms. When a respected senior behaves in a way that a young manager might otherwise question, it can set a tone for expected behavior that overrides classroom notions of ethics. Michael Hoffman* has told us of the studies at UniRoyal and at Pitney-Bowes that revealed large percentages of employees feeling this kind of pressure from above. *The Billion Dollar Bubble* dramatizes this kind of pressure and how difficult it is to resist. It is not at all clear how much can be done by schools alone to prepare managers for this aspect of reality.

Let me close with a story—a true story—that offers a more optimistic picture of business ethics. It concerns a manager who was bragging to a more senior executive about how he successfully handled a delicate moral problem that arose with one of his female employees. The manager had been informed by a bookkeeper who worked at the employee's bank that she had been making deposits far in excess of her salary. The manager investigated further and discovered that the employee was moonlighting in a most unprofessional profession. "What did you do about it?" asked the senior executive. "I fired her for immoral behavior," answered the manager. "Isn't that what you would have done?" "No," the senior executive replied, "I would have advised her to find another bank."

*Moderator, panel on "Educating Toward Ethical Responsibility."

Discussion

Question: I wonder whether either of you make use of something like the Association of Computing Machinery (ACM) code of ethics in your courses. Is that something that you teach or not?

Johnson: I make use of a discussion of the ethical code and the problems that usually arise over enforcement.

Question: Mr. Meldman, you said that IBM had a privacy ad. One of the interesting things about that particular ad is that it also matches their two testimonies before the federal government on privacy. Both times the discussion was narrowed down to the employee, and the ad says the same thing: item nine gives their employees privacy, and that's the beginning and end of the statement. But IBM has an impact far beyond its employees.

Meldman: I agree. Although I may have covered it up, I was attempting to be a little cynical when I mentioned that.

Question: No one has addressed the core problem of teaching ethics to students other than philosophy majors. I teach applied ethics in a management program, with others. I think all of us have con-cluded from our experience in that program that the people taking the kind of courses that we're talking about come to them with a background that has been characterized by the employment and manipulation of theories. Their training has enabled them to be decisive, to arrive at conclusions that, in effect, come out of the employment of the theory and the data. And they find that they have not been exposed to anything that enables them to be decisive with ethical problems in the same way that they have been able to take decisiveness for granted by the application of a formula and theory in areas they are familiar with. In spite of the fact that people going through those courses will concede at the end that they have had their ethical awareness enhanced—that yes, they are some-what more ethically sensitive—they're still faced with a sense of frustration and disappointment. Having known nothing, having gone into these courses with the word *ethics* connoting virtually nothing to them, they come out realizing that there is something a little bit phoney about it. And that's what I consider to be the Achil-les heel of applied ethics. Alasdair MacIntyre, of course, has been saying for a long time that this is something that we just have to accept; he considers it a permanent Achilles heel. I would be very interested in the observations of the panel members as to what their experience with this has been.

Johnson: In part, this is not our problem. It is very frustrating to me that my engineering students, for example, are taught that the theory is given and then you just solve the problem in terms of the theory. They are being mistaught because the theory *isn't* given. They're never told to question the theory, and they should be shown that theories in science and engineering are sometimes controversial.

Comment: That's part of the problem.

Johnson: Yes, but what I'm saying is that this is not something we have control over, except insofar as students express those frustra-tions. Then you can get them to see that things are not as simple in the technical disciplines as they think they are.

Meldman: Let me add that I'm not entirely sure that frustration per se is so bad. I don't mean that I think that we should try to avoid the issue with them. What I'm trying to figure out is how to get across to them that there is value in their having been left, in effect, in that new state of mind.

Johnson: I don't find that a problem. I think they know that there is value in that new state.

Meldman: And if they don't know that right away, chances are that they'll eventually find that out.

Comment: I think this enhances their awareness and sensitivity. We call it frustration, perhaps. It's painful, but I think immediately of the etymology of the word *scruple*. As I recall, it means "to have a pebble in one's shoe." And to be scrupulous is to have that slight discomfort. And perhaps, as educators, the best thing we can give them and do for students is to enhance and make them feel discomfort.

Johnson: To me, an attempt to try to find the easy solution, to make it seem simple, is, in a way, an attempt to shirk responsibility. We all have to face the fact that it is necessary to struggle with a moral decision.

Meldman: I feel that this is clearly a new challenge to the community of professional moral philosophers. Until the recent past when we started teaching these kinds of courses, we really were not significantly aware of this situation because we were teaching philosophy majors, who don't come to us in the same frame of mind.

Johnson: I agree.

Question: Do I understand that there is some consensus or code of ethics in the computer profession?

Johnson: I have two replies to that. I've only seen the proposed codes and I don't know if those are the ones that actually got passed. In any case, they're general and they still require some interpretation to apply to particular situations. But more importantly, too much emphasis on the code is misleading. Emphasizing the code is taking a legalistic approach. It implies that you have to behave in a certain way because your profession says so, rather than because the behavior is right or good.

Question: What do you mean by being legalistic?

Johnson: The code tells you that whether you like it or not, this is what your profession requires you to do. But there are certain things that your profession may not require you to do that you ought to do.

CHAPTER 5

Implications for Responsible Information Resource Management

Chapter 5A

Information Resource Management

*Elizabeth Byrne Adams**

Television, from time to time, exposes the public to the need for Information Resource Management. Such a situation occurred in 1981, as described in Figure 1. At the scene of the attempted assassination of President Reagan, data were captured and quickly relayed to television studios by reporters, photographers, bystanders, desk clerks, policemen, Secret Service agents, and all others in or around the area. The unedited data were then forwarded directly to Edwin Newman, Dan Rather, and Frank Reynolds, who had the unwieldly job of receiving it, processing it, and sharing it. These activities were conducted on camera, which required retrieval and dissemination activities to occur concurrently.

The information disseminated to the public included: the President was not shot; the President was shot; the bullet resided one inch from the heart; the bullet went through the shoulder; James Brady was dead; Brady was almost dead; Brady was not dead; the assassin was a Yale dropout, was twenty-two years old, was forty years old; there was a Nashville connection; the Secret Service was warned; the Secret Service denies a warning; letters from Jody Foster are significant; the President was undergoing open heart surgery at this moment; the President's family was coming; the President's family was not coming; General Haig was in control of the nation; and so forth.

*President, Management/Technology Interface, Inc.

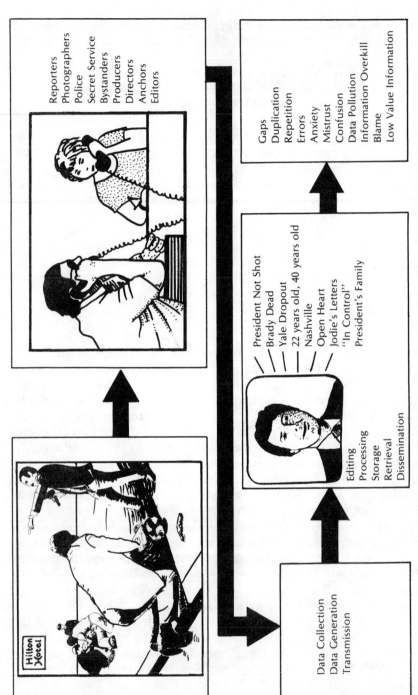

Reporters
Photographers
Police
Secret Service
Bystanders
Producers
Directors
Anchors
Editors

Gaps
Duplication
Repetition
Errors
Anxiety
Mistrust
Confusion
Data Pollution
Information Overkill
Blame
Low Value Information

President Not Shot
Brady Dead
Yale Dropout
22 years old, 40 years old
Nashville
Open Heart
Jodie's Letters
"In Control"
President's Family

Editing
Processing
Storage
Retrieval
Dissemination

Data Collection
Data Generation
Transmission

Figure 1. Information dissemination by television broadcasters in a crisis.

For several hours, the public was exposed to conflicting erroneous, repetitive, low-value, and generally unmanaged information. The missing link in a noteworthy fact-breaking news story covered by television with crisis management techniques is information resource management. And, unhappily, this missing link is *always* absent in most organizations today.

The equivalent to bystanders transmitting data at the scene of an emergency in public or private organizations includes computer installations, microcomputers, word-processing centers, and individuals processing information with paper and pencil. With all of these little chunks of information-handling going on throughout the organization, managers are soon deluged with too much information, unverified information, bad information, conflicting information, and late or inaccurate information. These problems are the problems of most managers in organizations today.

These are the problems that Information Resource Management (IRM) addresses by organizing information flows and information-handling technologies to accomplish organizational objectives effectively and efficiently. The implications of this statement are shown in Figure 2. In Pre-IRM, little packets of information are

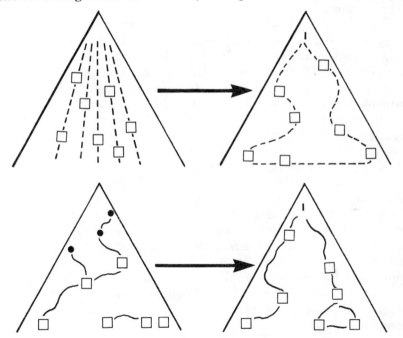

Figure 2. Pre- and post-IRM—integrating information handling technologies (bottom) and information flows (top).

processed in different functional areas, resulting in perhaps the computer facility, under the control of the comptroller, three word-processing centers reporting to the human resource director, and one reporting to the supply director. There might also be other information-handling activities in other areas, with no coordination, potential duplication, and probable repetition. If these diverse units forward information to one manager, then the probability and reality of conflicting data become very apparent. Information Resource Management, through policies and procedures, would coordinate the activities of these information-handling centers. This may not involve structural realignment, but does provide a policy umbrella.

The lower half of Figure 2 shows information flows, and implies meandering information systems, dead-ended information systems, and single-user information systems. These little fragments of information systems may or may not contribute to the goals and objectives of the organization. Information Resource Management, in the second part of the definition, proposes to integrate many of these information flows. This would result in coordinated information flows through electronic processing, mechanical processing, and manual processing. This latter point is significant in an age of office automation.

Introducing IRM (with these two themes) to an organization implies four areas of organizational impact. The first includes the view of regarding information as a resource similar to human resources, material resources, and financial resources. The second major area in the organization affected is current management principles and policies. To these must be added information-handling principles, policies, and procedures to provide overall management of information, whether in file folders, electronically stored in data bases, on magnetic tape, or transferred to clients electronically or by mail. The third area of impact is in the financial management of information. Organizations are not financially managing information, nor are they managing equipment expenditures. As the cost of information technologies decreases, equipment may be purchased from line manager's operating budgets and not centrally summarized as an information technology expense. The fourth area of organizational impact of IRM is the requirement for organizational change in a new component called the Information Resource Management Department, placed at the level of the organization where other significant resources are managed.

Information as a Resource. Information processed by a computer should be subject to the same standards, safeguards, and access limitations as that processed manually. Systems analysis and design should be geared toward integrating manual, mechanical, and electronic processing with trade-offs among them analyzed. Information as a resource requires resource management principles which include: (1) maximize the use of the resource; (2) minimize the cost of the resource; and (3) assign accountability for resource acquisition and use throughout the organization. In applying resource management principles to information, a need is established for an information plan that is integrated with the corporate or agency plan. Included in the information plan must be acquisition, processing, and ultimate use plans for both structured and unstructured information. Most previous system analyses and design efforts have dealt with structured information, but electronic mail and teleconferencing capabilities force the integration of these previously separate information areas.

Information Management. A primary requirement for "managing" is to know what it is we "manage." Most organizations do not have an inventory that includes manual, mechanical, and electronic information systems, data bases, software, files, and records. Before managing information one must identify the inventory of information in the form of meta-data (information about information). Policies concerning information ownership and custodianship must be formulated for different points in the processing cycle and clearly defined. These would preclude the misuse of information for power and establish accountability and right of access. Information management responsibility at a high level of the organization would enable integration of information, management style, and organizational structure. This may be the most significant failure in previous designs of information systems. Organizations succeed with a particular management style appropriate for its business and a certain structure that allows it to accomplish specific performances. Organizations need a unique information system to "fit" the management style and the organizational structure.

Integrated multimedia technologies are a primary consideration of the eighties. In previous decades the computer center manager managed the computer, the word-processing manager managed word processing, the records manager managed microfiche storage and retrieval, and others had responsibility for a category of information-handling equipment. Office automation unites these technologies and introduces the question: "Who is in charge of information, whether it comes up on a display device or on paper?"

Media independent information relates to storage design and the ability to "package" electronically stored information for the confirmed paper user, the confirmed CRT user, for the detail person, and for the "big-picture" person. In meeting all their needs, the bottom line is concern about the presence of information needed for the organization to accomplish its objectives. Formatting and delivery become secondary design points.

Information management should permit ongoing evaluation of information as its contribution to organizational development. Most previous attention to evaluation has been oriented toward utilization of nano-seconds (one billionth of a second). Nano-seconds are now trivial; effective information efficiently processed is what is significant.

Financial Management. Information has a cost composed of all the costs involved in the process of producing it. And yet in most organizations information is regarded as free and, as a minimum, only equipment costs of production are recorded. Financial management of information requires an accounting structure that has standard costs and variance costs for different information products. Line managers armed with the cost of information products can make trade-off decisions. Using costs as a yardstick, the user may assess the value of information. It should be the user—the line person—who judges the value of the provided information by his or her willingness to pay the costs of producing it.

Information Resource Management Organizational/Implementation. In all fields of human endeavor, activities were performed before principles for each field were in place. The development of management principles in finance, personnel, and material was an evolutionary process. Activities in each of these areas were pursued prior to and during the evolutionary development of principles. During the computer age of the last twenty-five years, information-handling activities have been expanding while Information Resource Management principles were and are evolving. Now many organizations are at the "readiness" level to begin Information Resource Management programs. This "readiness" includes: a certain amount of information handling, a level of information intensity, a dependence on information, and a degree of sophistication in information handling. Even at this readiness level, there are existing barriers to an information resource management program. These include personnel with vested interests in maintaining the status quo. New policies may be perceived as limiting for many in organizations. Therefore the introduction of policies that establish ground rules for ownership of information and custodianship followed by policies for information management is a way of phasing in better control over the information resource. Ultimately the need for an Information Resource Management Department, with an overview of information in the organization, can bridge the gaps between management style, organizational structure, and the information architecture.

A significant new set of management principles with widespread organizational impact must be accompanied by significant benefits. This is the reason why large organizations, in particular, throughout the world are embarking on Information Resource Management Programs. Among these benefits are: disciplined cost/benefit analyses, information reduction incentives, availability of information for upper management on demand, use of resource management principles for a newly identified organizational resource—information—and the safeguarding of information for organizational use. As organizations advance through the decade of the eighties, an established Information Resource Management Program will facilitate better decisions on meeting new information needs and selecting new technologies for information production processes.

The problems of too much information, too little information, conflicting information, unknown costs of information, and incorrect information that plague most organizations (dramatically demonstrated in news coverage during a national crisis) may be resolved by Information Resource Management. This is not, however, a panacea! An Information Resource Management Program has major organizational impact which must be anticipated.

Evolving Policy on Information Resources Management

W. Forest Horton*

I had planned to talk in detail about the specifics of Information Resources Management in the federal government. But what I'd rather do is to highlight that subject rather briefly and spend most of my time relating the subject of information resource management to the subject of this conference—business ethics.

The concept of IRM that Professor Elizabeth Adams has described so well has been a long time in coming. I don't think any single person or group can take credit for it. I was very fortunate to have been employed in the mid-seventies as the director of the information management study for the Commission on Federal Paperwork. That congressional commission was set up to study ways to reduce government paperwork and red tape burdens on the American public. For decades congressional committees had heard testimony from businesses, individuals, small institutions like this college, hospitals and other groups, on how they were being oppressed by too many government forms and too much red tape. And, indeed, in some instances, small companies were going out of business.

So the Commission came into being in late 1975, rose to a strength of some 200 staff members, and made some 600 recommendations

*Former Director, Federal Paperwork Commission

to the President and to Congress. I'm happy to report to you that it has "self-destructed" and turned back $1 million of unspent taxpayers' monies! Perhaps 95 percent of those recommendations were very specific—directed to a specific form, a specific report, or a specific record-keeping requirement or procedure. But the remaining 5 percent were, in my view, the most important because they addressed fundamental and far-reaching reforms which the Commission felt the government must undertake, that were aimed at the management of government paperwork and information.

The Commission rejected the historical posture taken by other study groups and commissions going all the way back to the 1800s— namely, that the problem was "too many pieces of paper." Rather, the Commission said, the *root* problem was that government at all levels *does not look upon information as a valued resource.* Nor does it apply the same disciplines in managing information as a resource that it applies to other resources—people, dollars, facilities, equipment, or even natural resources. From that basic posture, the Commission then evolved the concept of "Information Resources Management" or IRM, as it has come to be called.

I'm not going to repeat the information Professor Adams presented on IRM, but I might clarify a couple of points. First, the idea is basically a *macro* concept that works best with large organizations such as government agencies and big corporations—organizations that have very significant investments in their capital and operating investments in support of information flow, including information technologies. It doesn't work nearly as well with smaller organizations, and would probably be considered "overkill" when you get down to the level of a partnership or proprietorship kind of business.

Second, we're not talking about the *informal* information interchange process—that which goes on between two people, for example, at a meeting or conference or over the telephone. Instead, we're talking about the *formal* information interchange processes such as a reporting flow. That isn't to say that we can't or shouldn't improve informal information interchange processes. But I suspect that will take a lot more study and research by philosophers, behavioral and other social scientists, and others. IRM, in short, isn't going to solve that particular problem, although it can help.

Thirdly, we're talking about *organizational* contexts, not individual contexts. That distinction is important because if you don't make it, you quickly get into a First Amendment issue when people say, "You can't tell me what information I need; it is an invasion of my privacy"; or "That's an infringement of my rights . . ." Clearly we're not talking about that kind of thing. Rather, we're talking about the legitimate concern of stockholders in a corporate environment, who are entitled to the assurance that information technologies, like all resources, are efficiently used and effectively applied to bottom-line profit making; or, in the public sector, the comparable concern of taxpayers that their taxes are well spent for legitimate government functions that serve them. This quickly brings you to the concept of the *manager* and the information manager's functions.

One of the keys to the information manager's role is to act as a challenger or devil's advocate, to make sure that information requirements are "reasonable and rational." This doesn't mean that the information manager can or should dictate information needs; it does mean that in the appropriate forums—planning, budgeting, and so forth—he or she "asks the nasty questions" in the name of the head official. That role is *not* being played today in either the public or private sectors in any systematic manner.

In fact, in today's information environment I believe we have placed a very unfair burden on such people as the MIS director or the data processing officials to fulfill that kind of managerial/ devil's advocate role. This is because, in a sense, we have had a missing block, a missing role on the organizational charts: the one the Paperwork Commission suggested must now be filled by the information resources manager. We have complained that "users should become more involved in systems planning and design," or that "top management should become more involved and supportive." But these are hallow exhortations and admonishments that over two decades have proven virtually worthless.

We do currently have such an intermediary role (between the technologists/technicians and ultimate users) in the case of human resources, financial resources, physical resources, and material resources (the personnel director, the comptroller, the plant operations manager, and the inventory control manager, respectively). But we will not have one in the information area unless and until the Information Resources Manager gets appointed and put into place. I don't think it is fair to have asked the MIS director or the data processing manager to make judgments on the benefit/ cost issue or the "effectiveness" issue. That is a role the manager must play.

All of the IRM principles were finally mandated when the Congress passed PL 96–511 on December 11, 1980 (The Paperwork Reduction Act of 1980). It contains all of the provisions which Professor Adams laid out for you—the benefit/cost business, the valuation of information, the single official, and the so-called Federal Information Locator System (FILS). That system is intended to serve as a single, authoritative, central registry of all government in-flows of information from the public and flows between federal agencies. Eventually it may be expanded to internal agency information flows, reports to the Congress, and other information flows and holdings such as federal records holdings, federal evaluation studies, and others.

Unfortunately, because virtually everything in Washington, D.C. nowadays has been caught up in the Administration's overall economic reform "web," I don't think we're going to see very much happen with PL 96–511 for six months or a year, at the very least— possibly even longer, depending on how long it takes the government to get through this first priority of budget spending cuts and tax cuts. That law, like all others that don't have some direct connection with the President's overall economic reform program, will be put on the back, or middle, burner. One of the ironies is that the law *could* be used to a much greater advantage to further the Administration's aims; but the posture at the moment is more one of "cutting" than of "managing." For those of you who want to pursue this area in more detail, I suggest you get a copy of the law.

Now we come to the "controversial" part. The first issue is: Is the information manager going to be an information czar? Is he or she going to arrogate all of the power that abuse of the position could bring, and perhaps even aim to take over the company or government agency? Certainly there will be a spectrum of opportunities and risks here. At the one extreme will probably be the abuser/czars who attempt such a course. At the other extreme will be the benign resource managers who do the very minimum to upset the applecart. Hopefully in the middle will lie the bulk of the information managers. But I believe we should give the concept a chance, not reject it out of hand because of the potentials for this kind of abuse. For example, just because the comptroller may have "the keys to the vault" doesn't mean all comptrollers steal their companies blind. Nor does it mean that just because the personnel director is in a position to play favorites with people, appointments, transfers, promotions, and so on, that he or she does so. So I believe it will be with the information manager. The potential may be there, and we will undoubtedly have some incumbents who do abuse their authority. But I believe we should give the concept a chance.

Secondly, the censorship problem. Here the issue is different from the preceding one of arrogation of power. This problem is closer to the Orwellian "ministry of truth" fear that this new information management department is going to withhold information from us—to tell the divisions within the company or agency only what the IRM department wants to tell it. Once more, we will undoubtedly find some abusers in this category.

Third, the "executive privilege" issue, the withholding of information for "administrative convenience." This is somewhat like the first issue, but has a slightly different kind of abuse potential and relates more to hiding behind the national defense skirt when it is "inconvenient" for the information manager (or department) to release information to the public, to other internal divisions, to an administrative law proceeding, or to some other seeker.

Another issue is "secrecy in government." Again, this is closely related to several of the others, but there are important distinctions. This is the general allegation that the government collects too much information from too many citizens, businesses and other sources, and uses that information oftentimes "mischievously" for its own ends. It is the "big brother" syndrome—fear of government that chills the public and discourages it from trying to exercise rights and privileges.

There can be a collision between the government's need to have good information and the public's right to know. A balance between these two is embodied currently in such legislation as the Privacy Act and the Freedom of Information Act. Sharing information between government departments in the name of trying to reduce the total government information collection burdens on the public, and to avoid the collection of duplicative information, is about equal to the risks of fraudulent or inadvertent disclosure of sensitive, confidential information collected from a citizen or a business. The mood at the moment seems to be to limit the uses government makes of information to the stated purposes for which it was collected, and not cross these barriers. For example, IRS is not allowed to share tax information with other agencies except under very carefully prescribed circumstances; nor is the Census Bureau; nor are the regulatory commissions.

The last issue I want to raise might be called "technocracy gone wild." That is, the mindless, soulless government bureaucrat going to hide behind the information management concept as a way to buy more and more machines and equipment, and use the machines in ways that simply sound the bells and whistles rather than contribute to bottom-line effectiveness. Some information managers could become technocrats, seeing in machines a sinister opportunity to get control of the decision processes.

Now my point with regard to all of these areas, whether they are "ethics" issues in the technical sense of this conference or not, is that they are, in my view, all legitimate concerns. And as we now go about the serious business of introducing IRM, whether in the government à la PL 96-511, or in the private sector, we must be mindful of the potentials for abuse and, where possible, take preventive action in advance to minimize the opportunities for dysfunctional behaviors.

Discussion

Comment: Dr. Horton, I tried to point out earlier in the conference that you could hardly find a better example of the utter futility of trying to project the outcome of interaction between technology and society than George Orwell's *1984.* I doubt that there are many books published in this century that have had as much united impact on the psychological profile of our society. Orwell's premise was that the technology coming out of World War II, taking us into the post–World War II era, was going to play effectively into the hands of those people whose interest is in the maintenance of law and order. And we wholly neglected to give consideration to the fact that the people whose interest is the generation of social breakdown, discord, and anarchy are the more ingenious members of society, and are usually exercising more energy.

Horton: Did you want to know if a technocratic elite was going to emerge? Is that what you were concerned about?

Comment: I thought it was important for us to recognize that what we appear to be approaching is almost one hundred and eighty degrees out of phase with what Orwell was projecting.

Horton: My diagnosis of that, if you'll forgive me, is that I think those of us who keep talking "gloom and doom" on these issues centering around the abuse and misuse of computers, be it from a hardware standpoint alone, from the security standpoint, or from the privacy standpoint, have a kind of collective persecution complex. That is, we just don't seem to spend much time balancing the good impacts of technology with the bad ones. I'm sure I could, and I suspect Jim Emery could have given us a number of "horror stories" in such areas as social security and national defense. But there the benefits have also been very substantial indeed, and should counterbalance the horror stories. That is the way I read your question—I think we have all taken the "goods" for granted but have tended to ballyhoo the "bads."

Question: Isn't Information Resources Management a natural offshoot of the Management Information Systems (MIS) staff, or the operation of computer centers? After all, they've got all the technological stuff; they've got all the "toys." Why shouldn't they be the ones accountable for data use? I don't know who's going to control the access to it, but why is not Information Resources Management popular in MIS circles?

Horton: I really think that you are asking two questions. The first was, "Why don't we just rename the computer shop 'Information Resources Management' because that's where most of 'the stuff' is, the expensive stuff at any rate!" And the second question was, "Is that shop 'an offshoot' of MIS?" My response would be that during the decade of the eighties, we're going to see very clearly that the computer shop is *not* the only place where information is processed. It is processed throughout the organization, and we have just been paying more attention to the computerized systems because that is where the glamor is. I must say that after twenty-five years in the computer field, I've spent considerable time watching the machines, but not much time watching file folders go into drawers and get buried! There is a perspective and attitude among data processing and MIS people in the computer room that is quite different from that which is needed for Information Resources Management. There needs to be a deeper understanding of the direction of the organization, its goals, its objectives, how it is managed, what the company is in business for, and so forth. Frequently, by choice, people most involved with the computer shop are enthralled by the computer and the "bells and whistles" of hardware and software. Those who are not frequently leave and go into management information systems or into line management positions. But that's only the halfway house! There is a difference between MIS and IRM. And I see MIS as a part of Information Resources Management, rather than the reverse. Many corporations already have a vice president for management information or MIS. I see EDP, MIS, WP, microfiche, statistical activities—all of these activities under the same umbrella of an interdisciplinary IRM department. There are many technical questions here, but I don't think this is the appropriate time to go into all of them.

Question: What about GSA—can it become the focal IRM point in the federal government?

Horton: I think at some point the General Services Administration might try to change its colors and feathers and turn into more of an information management department. But there would have to be a lot of soul searching because GSA has traditionally been government's housekeeper.

Question: Could you be more specific as to the General Services Administration changes you see would be needed to move it to that kind of role?

Horton: I would have the staff (operational) role for much of the IRM policy development work done in GSA, but not under the current organizational setup. I think the Automated Data and Telecommunications Service (ADTS) is presently too narrowly conceived. And, too, the respective missions of the National Archives and Records and Service (NARS) and ADTS are not well sorted out. They need to be more completely rationalized. Nobody really is worrying about information content yet. GSA is still, I think, too much oriented toward individual information technology standards and guidelines and not focused enough on how they should be integrated.

Question: What about the National Telecommunications and Information Administration (NTIA); would you like to see more policy from them at this point?

Horton: Yes. Unfortunately I think NTIA has been spending most of its time on telecommunications, radio waves, and spectrum—the "hardware issues." I've been a little saddened that they haven't spent more time on what I call substantive information content policies.

CHAPTER 6

Computers and Privacy

*Arthur R. Miller**

I am here to talk to you very quietly and benignly and un-emotionally about a revolution. I call it the "Privacy Revolution." It is not a revolution fought with guns and tanks and planes. Rather, it is a revolution that has been going on in peoples' minds, in their feelings, in their attitudes, in their values and, what is very interesting for me as a lawyer, it is a revolution that has been going on within the legal system.

I use the word "revolution" in part because, as a lawyer, I am used to things happening very, very slowly. For example, one of my fields of interest happens to be the Law of Copyright—intellectual and artistic property. And in that field of the law, prior to 1978, we had been operating under a federal statute that was passed in 1909. Nobody thought it was important enough to address the fact that we had developed such things as motion pictures, the phonograph record industry, radio, television, computers, satellite communication. In the eyes of the law, it was enough to stumble along with a 1909 statute and make guesses as to what the law should do. So the word "revolution" as I am using it connotes the fact that, in less than twelve years, the legal system has become somewhat revolutionized in terms of this value we call the "right of privacy."

*Harvard Law School

Starting with the brouhaha about the National Data Center in about 1967, there has been a preoccupation, a focusing, an attention to various individual rights that we can bring under this amorphous umbrella known as the "right of privacy." And in that time, in the space of less than fifteen years, what has happened? Congress has enacted the Fair Credit Reporting Act. What is the Fair Credit Reporting Act? It is an act designed to protect the privacy, quality of information, and information flow in the consumer reporting industry, which embraces retail merchants, employers, and banks. In that same period Congress has enacted the Educational Privacy Act—the Buckley Amendment, which, for the first time in American history, represents a federal, and I underscore the word federal, presence on the campus, every campus, from primary school to postgraduate school, from public education to private education, from secular schools to religious schools. Every school in these United States is now under a congressionally enacted mandate to handle student files with a federal degree of care: what can be recorded, who can see it, auditing, document destruction policy, and a number of other things. I consider that statute, just by way of an aside, one of the most amazing pieces of legislation ever enacted in our federalist country, particularly since people like Strom Thurmond sit in key positions in the legislative branch. That's statute number two.

Statute number three is the Fair Information Practices Act of 1974, a massive federal statute controlling governmental data collection, governmental data maintenance, and governmental data dissemination. And there are little Fair Information Practices Acts that have sprouted, like weeds, at the state level throughout the country, Minnesota being the leader in that regard, Massachusetts being somewhat, but not too far, behind. These state statutes control state governmental information around the country. Those are three massive statutes in less than fifteen years.

In addition the United States Supreme Court, in *Roe v. Wade,* which is thought of as the Abortion Decision, recognized very clearly, very precisely, that the right of privacy in this country is constitutionally based. The Justices of the Supreme Court had a little bit of difficulty finding the privacy right in any particular part of the Constitution, so it is one of those "We-got-it-by-osmosis" kinds of things. But it's there; that's what the Justices say. True, it dealt with privacy of the body, and that is a unique type of privacy, but when you patch the Roe case together with other Supreme Court decisions dealing with freedom of ideology, freedom of association, freedom of protest, speech, and dissent, it all comes together as a broadly based right of privacy.

And we've had some amazing judicial decisions stemming from *Roe v. Wade.* Some of them are a bit humorous. You can look at pornography in the home, courtesy of your constitutional right of privacy. You can smoke pot in the home, courtesy of your constitutional right of privacy. On a serious note, you have a right to die. The New Jersey Supreme Court, in a decision involving Karen Ann Quinlan, allowed a hospital to take her off a respirator; this is a privacy case. Her right to privacy was held to embrace her right to die, which is being exercised for her by her parents. The right to die— a strange aspect of privacy. More germane to this conference, I suppose, is a California Supreme Court decision that says the constitutional right of privacy embraces freedom from governmental surveillance on the campus. Now I say again: from a legal perspective, this is a revolution. This is a legal revolution of the first order.

Why did this come about? Privacy is not a new problem. Privacy has been significant and threats to it have existed ever since two people existed. Adam and Eve probably had some need for privacy. The catalyst for the issue, of course, is the computer. We had barely any organized law of privacy prior to the computer. And if you start tracing it out, you begin to see the sensitivity about privacy starting to take a gradual and then escalating upward turn with the development of electronic data processing.

Part of it has been the expanded use of digits. I used to live in Brooklyn, New York. I am now told that, no, I didn't live in Brooklyn, New York, I lived in area code 212. I *think* I live in Cambridge. And, no, I am told I live in zip code number 02138. My telephone number used to be "Digby." Digby. That has a ring to it. Boy, I know a Digby when I see a Digby, but now I am told no, that old telephone number is now 344 or something or other. I used to think I was Arthur Miller. And now I'm told I'm really my Social Security Number. People don't like that. It may be a psychological problem rather than a factual one, but people think of themselves as humans, not code numbers. We have been brought up to think in terms of names and places and identifiers that are not a data or digit stream.

Think about it and imagine a high school Prom, the year 1984: a peach-fuzzed young man walks up to a young lady and says, "Hi, I'm 127-26-7378." And she blushes and replies, "Oh, it's so nice to meet you. I'm 097-12-8394." He shrinks back and says, "Funny, you don't look Jewish."

An allegory, nothing but an allegory. But it's the computer, the oversell of the computer, the constant movement to numerology in the sixties, that started the apprehension among all sorts of people, that somehow their right of privacy, their right of individuality, their right of autonomy, their sense of self, their notions of control over themselves and their fortunes, was threatened. This is what produced the reaction I am terming the Privacy Revolution. And privacy has deep roots in our society, although legally we haven't had to deal with it very much. We had, after all, in the eighteenth and nineteenth centuries an open frontier, a high rate of illiteracy, and no technology to record data. The mobility of American society prevented that data from being much of a threat to anyone. As Horace Greeley said, "Go West, young man, go West." I suspect he meant not only that there were economic opportunities on the frontier, but that it was a way to escape a bankruptcy record or a carping spouse back East. There was the ability to escape, there was no sense of closure in society. All of that is being threatened. To say to someone, "Go West, young man, go West," today is a cruel joke; the computer will have your files in San Francisco seven hours before you get there.

Let me try to describe these apprehensions. I am the first to admit that some of them are psychological, not objective. But some of them are very real and not mere figments of paranoid imaginations. Whatever their reality, these concerns exist. And they must be responded to because you don't tell a million, two million, five million people, or however many there are who are concerned about data collection in this society, "Oh, you're crazy, we're going to ignore you." Any data manager worth his or her salt must face the reality that there is a great deal of popular concern. And every public opinion poll taken in the last five or eight years shows a constant, upward swing in public attention to privacy. This used to be considered to be nothing but a white, middle-class value in the mid-sixties. The current surveying suggests this is no longer true, that over the last fifteen years there has been enormous attention to this issue. I think we can divide the apprehensions, the privacy concerns of people, into four discrete categories.

First is the cliché: We live in an information-based society. More and more institutions are collecting more and more data about more and more people and more and more of their activities. That's Apprehension Number One. There's too damn much data collection going on in this society. Too many people are asking too many questions and maintaining too many files. Stated in this way, it's a truism. I don't think anyone in his or her right mind will doubt the proposition that there's more data collection going on in this society than ever before. All you have to do is pull out the IRS Form 1040, which is what you fill out when you pay your taxes. To those of you who keep records, take out a 1040 from ten years ago and this year's, and lay the two IRS forms side by side. You'll be stunned at the increase in data collected from us by the IRS for the privilege of paying our taxes. The fine graining of the questions, the new categories of questions; any decent information scientist looking at somebody's 1040 can prepare a very extensive profile on that person. Not only do you have all of the taxpayer's financial dealings laid out, but you have all of the taxpayer's medical problems laid out if he takes the medical deduction; and you have all of the taxpayer's ideological and charitable associations laid out if he takes the charitable deduction.

Every time you get on an airplane, every time you rent a car, every time you check into a hotel, you create a file. Every time you apply for a job, every time you seek a credit card, every time you want insurance, every time you think you're eligible for a governmental benefit, you create a file. Those are not transient files. Most of them are permanent or semi-permanent files. The airline doesn't erase your travel record when you step off in Washington, D.C.; it is maintained and, increasingly, is a source of monitoring by the so-called organized crime strike forces to analyze travel patterns of suspects. And remember, those airline reservation services don't simply tell which flight you were on; if you stop and think about it, they obviously contain everybody else who was on that plane. If you're traveling with somebody, it will indicate that; if you've given a contact number at either end of your trip, it will show that; if you've rented a car or a hotel through your agent or the airline, it will show that as well. This type of file didn't exist ten years ago, before there was a thing called the computer. It is the computer that has enabled this constantly upward spiraling pattern of data collection in our society to exist. Why does the IRS ask so many questions? Why do social service agencies ask so many questions? Because they now have the technological capacity to record that data and, presumably, to use it.

I like to think of it as a variant on Parkinson's Law. Namely, any institution that gets a computer inevitably figures out ways to fill the capacity of that computer. And when it's filled the capacity of that computer, like in Parkinson's Law, it goes out and gets itself another computer. And since organizational power in so many parts of our society has as its vortex the computer and the ability to control and manage the computer, it is like a dog constantly chasing its tail.

You find the most incredible quantities of data collected. Why? Because the capacity to store it exists. Why? Because somebody always says, "Gee, since we're doing a survey, we might as well ask these additional questions because someday we might need the information." That seems to be the wail of the longitudinal researcher. "We might as well ask that, we might as well ask this, we might as well ask this," and so on. The net result is: surveys multiply, elongate, and people have the overwhelming sense that they are being subjected to more and more information extractions—to use the dental analogy—as part of daily life in this country. And many of them don't like it. But worse, in my judgment, is that many people are getting used to it because we're becoming anesthetized to any sense of individuality about our informational profile. And that's Apprehension Number One.

Apprehension Number Two is also, I think, a truism. It's this: more and more decisions about us are being made on the basis of files. And when I use the word "files" I'm talking about manila files as well as computer files. Decision making is less and less based on a face-to-face dynamic. We don't deal, as we once did on the frontier and in the rural environment at the turn of the century, across the table with a banker, or a credit grantor, or an admissions office, or a governmental agency. Today the question is whether your file falls within the right decision-making parameter—what a fateful word! If you want to get credit, to get a job, to get insurance, or to get a benefit, you are increasingly dependent on what is in the files; more and more decision-making occurs by file. The phenomenon surrounds us. And even though we are sitting here in the gentility of an academic community, we are not free of it. Have you ever considered how you get into many professional schools these days?

Let's take a big, hypothetical professional school. Perhaps one that gets 8,000 applications a year. There can't possibly be any face-to-face dynamic. So what happens? Let's take an average twenty-two or twenty-three-year-old breathing, aspiring, fresh, flesh and blood college senior, and assume he or she wants to go to law school. After getting an application from our hypothetical school our senior sits, night after night, filling out the forms recording the events of his or her twenty-two years, including the essay, "Why I Want to Go to Law School" or "The Greatest Book I Ever Read." Our applicant sits there, night after night, writing part fact, part fiction. A tear drops here, a whimsical smile there. But the entire life of that applicant is embodied in that application form, which is then entrusted to the United States postal system and eventually, we hope, comes to our hypothetical law school. Then, our twenty-two-year-old breathing applicant, now represented by the application of that applicant, is opened up, a few entries made in books at the admissions office, and the forms are shot off, you know where? To the Educational Testing Service in New Jersey.

Upon arriving at ETS it is handed over to the data processors who immediately take the transcript and keypunch it into the machine. Now, this is not just an ordinary machine. It is a very sophisticated computer because if the school is at all adept at the admissions process, there is a program in ETS's computer that *adjusts* the transcript. You realize that they don't just "adjust the transcript," because there's a twenty-two-year-old in back of that transcript. It's the applicant who is being adjusted, essentially lobotimized. The adjustments take the form of kicking out certain courses— perhaps Military Science or Music Appreciation—and a new grade point average is computed. The transcript is then further adjusted because many law schools have developed an experience base showing how students from numerous undergraduate institutions perform at their school. The truth is that an "A" average from Cal Tech is very different from an "A" average from Siwash U, at least as far as admissions officers are concerned. So this marvelous computer program augments or discounts the already adjusted transcript, depending on where that applicant went to school.

So let's take a simple example—an adjusted grade point average, according to ETS's computer, of 3.5. This is then multiplied by an arbitrary weighting number, let's say 200, producing 700. To which is added the applicant's Law School Aptitude Test grade. The Law School Aptitude Test is thought by many to be another one of society's depersonalizations. They believe it is somebody's cruel joke as to what characteristics go into making a lawyer because it was not prepared by lawyers, and most lawyers would laugh at it if they saw it. In any event, let's take another simple number—700 on the Law School Aptitude Test. So we have an adjusted grade point average weighted to 700, and we have a Law School Aptitude Test score of 700. We now have what is euphemistically called a Predictor Index Score of 1400, which is supposed to indicate whether this human being can make it at the law school. ETS sends the number 1400 back to the admissions office of the hypothetical law school.

Let's see where we are. We have taken the twenty-two-year-old college senior, reduced him or her to a formal application, and then taken the formal application and reduced it to a number—1400. But we're not done. When the number 1400 arrives at the admissions office it is taken by some functionary over to a wall chart. A floor to ceiling wall chart—a scattergram. And where the axes show a Predictor Index Score of 1400, our admissions office functionary carefully puts a dot. Our twenty-two-year-old aspiring, flesh and blood applicant is now a fly speck, a dot on the wall.

Then about this time every year, the high priests and priestesses of the admissions office, garbed in the appropriate dress, engage in something like a crypto-religious rite of spring. They go to the great wall chart, as one would go to the Oracle at Delphi, and they draw two parallel lines. Now, if you, or should I say your dot, appears above the top line, you are automatically admitted. If your dot appears below the bottom of the two lines, you are automatically rejected. If your dot appears between the two lines, you are in a hold category and someone probably will go to the manila folders and see if they can differentiate you, rather, your dot, from someone else's dot. In all three cases, the applicant's admit, reject, or hold letter is produced by computer.

People don't like that kind of decision making. It may be necessary in a mass society such as ours, but that doesn't make people like it any more. It takes much of the humanity out of life. It makes one feel as if he or she is completely at the mercy of the data handlers. How does an individual know what the so-called "parameters" of decision making are, the criteria of admission or rejection? How does the individual know which elements in the data stream are germane and which are irrelevant to the decision maker? How does the individual even know that the decision maker has the right data, that it is factual, that it is accurate, current, and verified, not hearsay or gossip, that it has been programmed correctly? I often worry that my credit files around the country are littered with the debris of other Arthur Millers. That's Apprehension Number Two.

And now Number Three. We have talked about increased data collection, we have talked about decision making by data. Now I want to talk about the risks of "data out of context." And I am not talking about misplaced digits or errors in the data. I am talking about the fact that data generally is created in an environment, for a purpose, by a group with particular standards relating to its objectives. The police have standards in generating arrest records. Universities have standards in establishing grading scales. The military has standards in terms of efficiency reports on its personnel. Every organization that generates data does so for a purpose, and under standards germane to it.

And that is perfectly acceptable in a data environment in which the information is static: it is generated, posted, stored, and doesn't move. But we know that is not reality in the 1980s. The computer and communications technology have completely obliterated any time or space limitation on data movement during the last twenty years. There is no such thing as localized data anymore. We can shoot data to the moon and back in seconds. We bring television signals in from Teheran in seconds. We send credit reports transcontinentally in seconds. And we can send medical data transcontinentally or intercontinentally in seconds. Scientists have placed a lot of emphasis on the time-space configuration of data movement and data transfer. But thus far very little consideration has been given to the fact that when you move data from one context to another, there is no reason to believe that the receiver has the foggiest notions of the purpose, the standards, or the inferences to be drawn from that data, because he, she or it didn't generate it and may be 8,000 miles away from the point of initiation. That's what I mean by "data out of context." The fact is that our great technologies can make the data available anywhere, but no one has educated people to understand the data beyond the superficialities of "Oh, it's an A" or "Oh, he's been arrested" or "Oh, he has this physical characteristic." Maybe that particular physical characteristic was germane to the employer that created the file because the company operates in a high dust-producing environment, but it's totally irrelevant for working in a bank 3,000 miles away or for granting credit.

Let me give you an example—arrest records. They circulate in most parts of this country freely. Not, supposedly, in Massachusetts; Massachusetts is one of the few states in the nation that has put limitations on the movement of criminal justice information. But, generally speaking, arrest records circulate. Now if they only circulated within the law enforcement community, that would be one thing. We can more or less take the risk that law officers, whether they be in Los Angeles or Boston, view life from much the same perspective. They know why an arrest file is generated, what it means, and why a particular entry was made.

But no one in this room should have any doubt as to the ability to move arrest information beyond the law enforcement community. I trust you've all been reading the newspapers and watching television, where every criminal justice entry relating to Mr. Hinckley has been recounted for days. Indeed, all that information was generated and publicized within hours of the offense. To the extent that the law enforcement community needs the technological capacity to move information nationally or internationally to promote law and order, I am with them. That sounds terrific to me. I don't want a Massachusetts State Trooper's head blown off on the turnpike because he doesn't know he has stopped someone more dangerous than a speeder, somebody who has outstanding warrants for bank robbery, murder, and arson. There are things he can check out through his vehicles communications gear, which is tied to the computer terminal at headquarters. And certainly I want the Secret Service, the FBI, and all the rest to find out about Mr. Hinckley within minutes of the shooting of the President. The crime is that they didn't find out about Mr. Hinckley before, but that's another story.

You've all seen the program *The FBI* on television—the original with Efrem Zimbalist, Jr., as Inspector Erskine. They're hot on the trail of some suspect and he says to another neatly dressed, brush-cut agent: "Check him out in NCIC." Well, NCIC isn't the figment of television's imagination. NCIC is the National Crime Information Center. It is an on-line computer-based system that makes available all arrest records and outstanding warrants to anyone with a terminal attached to NCIC, and there are thousands of those terminals throughout the nation.

However, its uses go beyond law enforcement. To be a beautician in Florida, you get checked out in NCIC; to be a croupier in Vegas, you get checked out in NCIC. Remember, these are mostly arrest records. But an arrest is a charge, it is proof of nothing, a fact that seemingly has escaped many employers in this country. "Have you ever been arrested?" This strikes me as an impermissible question, yet the answer is coming out of NCIC. The statistics show that almost 40 percent of the data in NCIC are raw arrest records, not convictions. Yet they are on preemployment investigations and credit checks and insurance inquiries. That is data out of context.

Let me give you some real rap sheets. Arrested: June 5th, 1943. Charge: Felony. Indicted. Tried: January 4th, 1944. Convicted. Sentenced: Three years, Leavenworth. Served: Six months, probation. That's a rap sheet; that's the data stream that comes across that terminal in Podunk. In fact, that's an interesting rap sheet because it is the rap sheet of a *convicted* felon. Remember, 80 percent of them just say "Arrested." No disposition data is provided and the subject may have been exonerated. So there you are, sitting in the great corporate empire in the sky, deciding whether this "convicted felon" is to get a job. Better safe than sorry, you might say, reject him, and call for the next applicant. Do you stop to ask what the crime was? It's not on that data stream. The reality is that it was conscientious objection, World War II. And the conviction was under a standard since struck down as unconstitutional in the Muhammed Ali case. The applicant really isn't a felon at all. Oh well, next file.

I'll give you another one a little closer to home, looking around this room. Arrested: Meridian, Mississippi, April 5, 1957. Charge: Criminal Trespass. Convicted. Sentenced: Six months probation. Boy, that's a bad apple. That's one of those violent vandal kids, right? No job for that punk. Criminal trespass sounds bad! But it really was a Civil Rights demonstration; the conviction was reversed on appeal as being an impermissible intrusion on First Amendment protected conduct. How are you going to know that? I am not blaming you for not knowing it. All I am pointing out is the danger of relying on foreign data without any sense of what it means.

Let me describe another phenomenon. In the late sixties there was a back-office crunch in the brokerage houses of Wall Street. What that meant was that the trading pace exceeded the capacity to handle the transactions. So a number of stock certificates disappeared. To this day we don't know whether it was just accounting errors, whether they were misplaced, or whether there was massive fraud or embezzlement. The New York State Legislature reacted, as all legislatures, all policymakers, do in a crisis; they panicked. They passed a statute. From now on, the statute provided, before anyone could work in the brokerage industry, he or she had to go through Arrest Record Clearance. That starts with fingerprinting, just like they do, you know, in those bad countries. Then they check the prints out in NYSIIS. NYSIIS isn't so nice. It's the New York State Intelligence and Investigation Service; this is a computer system, New York's equivalent to the FBI's NCIC. If the system showed an arrest, the odds were you didn't get the job. Better safe than sorry (think in terms of the mentality of the bureaucrats who make the decisions on hiring stock boys or girls and messengers).

Now let me give you a few statistics. I hate statistics but occasionally they are illuminating. If you're black, if you're male, if you're a late teenager (eighteen or nineteen), if you come out of Bedford-Stuyvesant or Harlem in the City of New York, the odds are between eight in ten and nine in ten you have an arrest record—not a conviction record, an arrest record. Inner-city police know how to keep the lid on in the summer—a little sweep down 125th Street. Maybe the kids are just rolling craps in the alley, but take them in, just keep them off the street, book them, throw them back out when it's late enough at night so they'll just go home. Better safe than sorry. Eight out of ten, nine out of ten teenage black males have an arrest record in the City of New York. How are they going to get jobs in the securities industry? What happened to our commitment to equal opportunity in employment? The right hand doesn't know what the left hand is doing. That is data out of context.

Fourth Apprehension. This, in my humble judgment, is the most important one of them all because it goes to the roots of what you want in a democratic society. It is the apprehension about governmental data collection which creates the feeling that "the government knows too much about me"; that I am no longer in control of my informational profile; that to do anything with the government involves a data extraction—whether it's paying my taxes, getting a mortgage on a house, or applying for some governmental benefit. And add to the general phenomenon of increasing data collection by governmental agencies the picture of domestic surveillance by the government, as we had during the Viet Nam War, when the Quakers were infiltrated, let alone the SDS, and the crazies. At that time if you went to a rally, you ran the risk of being photographed and posted in a Rogue's Gallery. If you signed a petition, there was a pretty good chance that every name on that petition would go into some file, somewhere.

Ask yourself whether that type of data collection and surveillance is at all consistent with notions of democracy and freedom, let alone consistent with the expressed constitutional guarantees of free speech, assembly, protest, and dissent set out in the First Amendment to the Constitution. Why do I have to be posted in a file just because I sign a petition about Viet Nam? Or about the abolition of the Legal Services Corporation? Or on nuclear power? Why does my government take down that fact and how are they going to use it? That is the apprehension.

We tend to react badly in crisis. Every civil liberties mistake we have made in our history was made at a time of crisis: the Alien and Sedition Laws in 1798, the suspension of the Writ of Habeas Corpus during the Civil War, the imprisonment of the Japanese-American population during World War II, the McCarthy Era, the activation of the domestic military intelligence network by President Johnson, who was reacting to the inner city riots, the Enemies List prepared by Mr. Nixon. These are all abuses of our civil liberties *justified* because of a "crisis."

Now let's look at a certain, I think fairly obvious, psychological fact. Many of us are emotional Spartans; we don't give a damn about having our names taken, our pictures taken. If we believe something, we will pursue that cause, that belief, that ideology, whatever. But certainly many of us are not. Countless among us may be deterred from going to a rally if we believe that our name or our picture will be taken and put into a file, especially since we don't have the foggiest notion what that file will be used for and by whom. What we are talking about is what some psychologists refer to as the Record Prison Syndrome: people surrounded by files and data collection begin to lose sense of themselves as individuals; they believe that they are in a record prison themselves; they begin to react by always wanting the records to reflect well on them; and then they act accordingly. And you know what those words "act accordingly" amount to? They describe behavior modification. If you are not going to go to the rally because you don't want to run the risk of looking bad in the government's eyes, you have had your behavior modified by your government. And that is exactly why, when the FBI decided to engage in surveillance of the Quakers, they did it overtly. I used to think it was the *covert* surveillance that was the big problem. It turns out that *overt* surveillance is just as threatening.

The FBI may have done it to the Beacon Press following the publication of *The Pentagon Papers;* they come into Boston with this big campaign, "We're going to find out how the papers got to the Beacon Press." Knowledgeable people say they already knew how they got to the Beacon Press. Certainly many people knew where Dan Ellsberg was at that point. Big headlines in the *Globe:* "FBI to Examine Financial Records of the Beacon Press," and at that time it was part of the Universalist-Unitarian Church. This may sound crazy to you, but people stopped going to church. Attendance at the churches dropped. Contributions, other than in cash, dried up for months. That's behavior modification. That isn't consistent with anything I know about what this country is supposed to be all about. I hate to use the image of *1984,* but it's apt. Surveillance is Big Brother on the television screen, watching us. You know what the true, the ultimate, lesson of *1984* and its notion of Big Brother on the television screen is? It's that it doesn't matter whether there actually is a Big Brother on the television screen. It doesn't matter at all whether somebody is, in fact, watching you. The only thing that matters is that you *think* that there's somebody watching you. You'll do the rest to yourself. We're human beings; we react. We don't even know we're reacting, that we are modifying our behavior.

Privacy Revolution. That is why public consciousness about privacy is as high as it is right now. And this is not a kooky phenomenon; this is not a Howard Hughes–Greta Garbo syndrome; this is not a lefty, ACLU, civil liberties phenomenon. I remind you of the cosponsorship of the Federal Fair Information Practices Act: Ed Koch and Barry Goldwater, Jr. Ed Koch, then the Liberal Democrat from New York and Barry Goldwater, Jr., the ultra-conservative Congressman from Orange County, California. That is a marriage made in heaven. Why? For the liberal, it's civil liberties, for the conservative, it's anti–big government philosophy.

There are five themes. First, I think increasingly we are beginning to recognize an important ethical and moral principle: if you can't get people's attention through basic ethics and morality, eventually you begin to legislate. I think we are recognizing the proposition that every data collector and every data handler and user in our society owes what the law calls a fiduciary obligation— which you can translate into a humanistic notion of good faith, fair dealing—to the data subject. The obligation applies whether you're talking about a credit data operation, a bank, an employer, a university, a hospital, a governmental agency. The information handler *owes* the subject a duty of care to make sure that the information is germane, that it is current, and that it is verified. And we've already had cases in the courts about how we make people who are not satisfying that fiduciary obligation compensate those who are injured. That is theme Number One.

Theme Number Two: Increasingly I think we are seeing recognition of a notion that certain kinds of information should not be collected at all. AT ALL. Don't collect it even though the longitudinal researchers say they might be interested in the data eight years down the pike. Some of it is fairly obvious: political affiliation, religious association, ideology. More and more, people are beginning to understand that you must have a pretty good reason for encroaching on those areas of individual privacy. People are beginning to think about what it is they *really* need to know, as opposed to what it is they'd *like* to know, let alone what they might have some morbid curiosity about.

Principle Number Three is primarily administrative and technological. Namely, it's the notion that systems require safeguards. We will never achieve fail-safe; there has never been a lock without a key. But that does not mean that we cannot reduce the possibility of breaches of confidentiality. We must use access coding audit trails, have ombudsmen, indoctrinate data handlers as to the values of privacy and the importance of confidentiality. I, for one, am much more inclined to give information when, in return, I get a pledge of confidentiality that I can rely on. This objective requires a combination of technological, administrative, and educational efforts.

The Fourth Theme is almost a universal right now, probably the most advanced of all of these principles. It is the recognition of the right of the data subject to gain access to his or her own file.

The data subject used to be the one person excluded from the file. Psychologically that is foolish in terms of an institution's relationship with that individual. It is foolish because a data collector or user has no interest in having bad information, and who is in a better position to make sure a file is accurate than the data subject? I view this as almost a due process right, certainly in the context of relationships with governmental agencies. I have a due process right to see what you've got on me and to correct it if it is wrong. To be sure, there is a lot of mindless chatter about the system's privacy, or, "Oh no, we can't tell him about his mental condition. He's going to jump out of the fifth floor." That is the reaction of part of the medical fraternity. The answer to that is easy: "How many people have jumped out of the fifth floor window lately upon seeing their file?" Moreover, using a third party to screen the data is the obvious solution in any situation in which there is a legitimate reason not to let the actual data subject see the file; there is always an intermediary who can verify the information.

Finally, the Fifth Theme. In many ways information has a life cycle. You can be very anthropomorphic about it. Information is born, just the way we are, when it's generated; it grows, as we do; it gets married to other files, and, like at least half the population, information gets divorced when you separate bits of information and scatter them in different directions; and information, like all of us, gets older, and older. But unlike us, information *never* seems to die. That's the Fifth Principle: death to information! We have got to stop being so anal retentive. We must begin to get information out of operating systems and at least into the archives; some of it must be expunged. And I know that word "expungement" just drives the historians, and the anthropologists, and the archivists up the wall. But at least get it out of the operating systems so that it doesn't sit there like an informational time bomb.

I recognize that I have spoken rather sharply about this subject. It's a subject I feel strongly about. And I'm always reminded of a line by e e cummings, the great American poet—"progress is a comfortable disease." We all get benefits from data technology. We could not run our Social Security system without it. (We may not be able to run it with it, but at least we have a fighting chance!) We could not enjoy the benefits of high-speed communication and high-speed transportation, flying would be an infinitely more hazardous job if we didn't have data technology. We receive wonderful benefits from the computer. And progress is a terribly comfortable disease because we tend to become anesthetized to the fact that, like any technology humankind has ever come up with, from fire to the wheel to the internal combustion engine, the computer has deleterious side effects. And I am not here as a nineteenth-century Luddite arguing that we should axe the machines but, rather simply, to talk about the need to engage in the classic cost-benefit, plus and minus analysis with regard to computer and information technology that we use in other contexts. Maximize its social utility, yes, but minimize its deleterious side effects. Above all, keep a weather eye out for the information managers because that is a subculture all to itself that will proceed down life's pathway to the beat of its own drummer, not necessarily in pursuit of society's best overall interests. I am not suggesting they are malevolent. Everyone in life is mission oriented and sees the world through their own eyes. And all of us are astigmatic to some degree. So let's not wake up one day and find that the information-management subculture is so much in control of the technology that they, in effect, are making decisions about people in the name of what's good for the data system. (How many times have human practices been adjusted to the fact that the machine only takes five digits, or something like that?) Because if we do wake up one day and find that kind of mentality at the wheel of the ship of state, we will have a dictatorship of dossiers and data banks, rather than hobnail boots. But don't kid yourselves, it will still be a dictatorship.

Discussion

Question: Picking up on what you said about the fiduciary relationship of the computer manager or computer person and putting that together with what has been reported, one of the things that bothers me about that legislation is that it's only when you inquire about whether or not information about you is in the bank that they are obligated to tell you or show you. But in essence this seems to be totally inadequate because in order to find out whether or not this information is there, I have to write a bunch of long letters. Shouldn't the person who maintains a data bank be obligated, in good faith, to inform you that they've got information about you?

Miller: There are at least two immediate answers to that. First, as you can imagine, any piece of legislature is a vectoring of forces, and the people upon whom privacy legislation has been imposed have been fighting it tooth and nail. When you get into the legislative environment and you say to a consumer reporting agency, a credit bank, "Hey! You're going to have to give notice to every person you open a file on, and give them notice every time there's a change in the file," they immediately go to "the-foundations-of-the-republic-are-crumbling" type of argument—namely, that you have put such an administrative burden on us that we cannot operate, we will die, and everybody in society will lose the benefit of the credit environment. Or, they will say, "The cost of doing that is going to double the cost of credit screening, which will double the cost of borrowing money." So, in a sense, it was a pragmatic judgment to abandon the notion of automatic notice to each person every time a file was created. On a cost-benefit analysis, creating those files was thought to be unworkable.

Notice is a wonderful right in the abstract. The truth of the matter is that for every hundred notices you send out, maybe one, two, or three people will actually look at it. This fact coupled with the cost of sending the notice was enough to scuttle it.

Question: Some of the Europeans, particularly the Scandinavians, have been extremely active in legislating for protection of privacy. Do you think that will be the way with Americans in the future?

Miller: Probably the perfect example is found in Sweden. The Swedish data protection act is the first in the world; it is probably among the most comprehensive, and is a relatively benign law. We should bear in mind that Sweden has a basically homogeneous population. It is not as fractured as American society with alienated subcultures. In addition, it has had over a hundred years of peace; its citizens have had several centuries of rather good relations with the government. In other words, the people place a great deal of faith in the Swedish government and their society. It is, for all practical purposes, a socialist state, heavily dependent upon government largesse, and in that kind of environment you can develop information legislation a lot more easily than you can in a country like the United States. That is simply by way of explanation of "Why the Swedes?"

My own judgment as to what is going on in the United States right now is that we are in a holding pattern. We have had, as I said, fifteen years of intense activity. We are now unlikely, particularly given the cost-conscious, anti-regulation political climate of the day, to escalate the privacy revolution to a second stage, which would have to go after such things as corporations, the medical profession, the hospital industry, and the insurance industry. What I see happening is a ten- or fifteen-year period of experience building up under the existing regime with a fresh look being taken at that time. The climate just wouldn't tolerate increased regulation of the private sector now.

I see that also with the judiciary, by the way. The U.S. Supreme

Court has taken some basic steps in recognizing privacy. But since the decision in *Roe v. Wade,* the basic abortion case, it has really not moved in the field of informational privacy. The U.S. Supreme Court seems to be in a holding pattern also. (And one of the ironies of the day is that if you really want to push for civil rights or civil liberties, whether in the area of environment, race, sex, or privacy, you are much better off at the state level in many parts of this country.) I think we are in a digestive pattern now of trying to absorb everything that has happened over the last decade.

Question: The post office is about to put out twenty million zip codes; there are just under eighty million addresses in the United States. That would work out to one zip code for every four of us. More likely, there would be about a hundred people in one zip code area. If this were enacted, it would have a massive impact on data generation. I'm assuming everyone in the room here would be forced to take into consideration the new data generation. I see nothing in print that leads me to believe that very much consideration of privacy is being given.

Miller: I think that's right. I think the debate—and that dignifies it—about the nine-digit zip has been totally oblivious to privacy thus far. It is just the way, in its formative stage, that the debate over the National Data Center took place in the mid-sixties. That went on with total obliviousness to the potential privacy implications of that proposal. By the way, the social security number probably is not an effective individualized identifier, and you could go to a nine-digit zip and convert it into a personal identification number without too much further work. But nobody seems to be talking about it. What you see in the media is more humorous than serious.

Question: Is there any legislation giving employees the right of access to their files in their country?

Miller: There were proposals by the President's National Commission to Study Privacy that went in that direction, but I don't know of any legislation that is likely to succeed. Just a little footnote to that: I do get some sense that labor unions are beginning to see the privacy issue as something that is germane to the labor-management dynamic. But as I said a few minutes ago, I don't think it's realistic to anticipate federal legislation on private company employment files.

Comment: Just in the larger context, in Belgium the Royal Decree of 1973 not only gives to works councils the right to company data but also, through work councils, gives employees the right to their own personnel files, a right which exists through codetermination legislation in Germany, in the Netherlands, in Sweden, Denmark, and Norway already. Whether it will come in the States, in an environment which is moving away from regulation, is still an open question. The models are in place, and the strongest one is the Royal Decree of 1973 in Belgium.

Comment: I agree with you that one of the toughest legislative issues arises when you propose that people have access to all their data, including medical data. And the medical establishment always contends that this could cause anxiety that would be damaging to patients' life or health. However, there was one study in a psychiatric hospital where patients and staff shared the records, and the results were that nobody was harmed by having access to their psychiatric data. These patients were hospitalized; no one was harmed, and the staff even decided that some patients benefited from having a frank discussion of their condition, which was stirred by having access to files.

Question: The business community came out badly on several ethical counts in some of our discussions. What sort of ethical considerations are built into the work that is done now at Harvard in educating lawyers?

Miller: I just had a *déjà vu* of an appearance I made on the Phil Donahue Show recently, which was one hour of "When-will-you-stop-beating-your-wife?" People always seem to take the opportunity to list the number of lawyers involved in Watergate. If the law schools today are much more attentive to ethical problems, it's called professional responsibility in our context. The truth is that Watergate caused the profession a great deal of anxiety, and a great deal of pressure was put on the academic side of the legal profession by the American Bar Association. And a lot of pressure was internally generated to try and deal with problems of ethics, morality, and social responsibility inside the legal curriculum.

Most law schools today have a required course or at least one elective in ethics as such, or pursue these matters as part of one of the traditional courses, such as criminal law, which is earmarked as a professional responsibility course. One of the basic objectives is to make the law student see every major issue in criminal law not simply from the adversarial model perspective, but also from ethical, moral, and social responsibility perspectives. This is a formal requirement that now exists in every first-class law school I can think of. Beyond that I can only speak autobiographically and by projection to those colleagues in the law-teaching business I am close to. I think there is a greater sense on the part of the individual law teacher that his or her job includes the teaching of professionalism—and not simply the rule of land transfer or the rule of making a tort liability but, for example, the professionalism of how you represent clients in a disadvantaged environment. Each of us to some degree has augmented our own courses with discussions about what I loosely call professionalism. Again, I am just being autobiographical at this point, inferring from the way I teach my basic course in court procedure these days. I teach it much more from the perspective of the system and the system's needs, namely, society and society's needs, rather than purely as an exercise in the advocate's role. So I think a lot has been done educationally. Whether between the ages of twenty-two and thirty, and therefore are reasonably formed ethically, is, of course, uncertain.

Question: What do you think about what the complexities of the computing issue are doing to court procedure? In *IBM v. Memorex,* an antitrust case, the judge decided that the jury was incompetent to decide what was going on. There are some very complex issues out there, and I wonder if you feel that perhaps the complexities are going over the heads of the juries.

Miller: The answer is yes and no. There is no doubt that any new technology presents the legal system with enormous new challenges and questions. The issue of whether software should be copyrightable or patentable is a public policy decision. The problem is not unique to the computer. The same kinds of problems occur with atomic energy and satellite communication. With regard to the issues of high technology that come into the courts for litigation, yes, you're dealing, by definition, with judges and juries who reached maturation in the generation before the technology. So you've got at least a generation of catch-up before your judges begin to live on intimate terms with the computer—which they're doing now because there's a computer-based legal research system that is available in most of the major courts in the country. Yes, they have difficulty; they have always had difficulty. They had difficulty when Watt developed the steam engine; they had difficulty, I am sure, when the first oxcart ran somebody down on the public highway.

That's inherent in the movement of society. We have always lived with the curious notion that one of the bastions of generalism in our society is the judge. But once you start making judges specialists, you are losing all sorts of human and social dimensions. You just have to bite the bullet and say, "Hey, you, generalist judge! You've seen life from beginning to end! I'll trust you with this software question, or antitrust question, rather than give it to a blindered telescopic-sighted specialist in economics or in computer technology!" That is a value judgement we have made.

A footnote: There is a raging controversy in this country about the jury system; I'm interested that you put your finger on it. We have been committed in this country since 1791 to lay justice through the jury system; trial by peers is in our Constitution. And now we've reached 1981 and people ask: "How can you give a lay group of twelve people, twelve average people, twelve Johnny Carson viewers, problems of high technology? And some courts say that they're not going to give these problems to the jury because they are beyond the jury's competence. Other judges take the position that it is in the Constitution, and we have no power to override the Constitution. The United States Supreme Court is going to resolve this issue one day.

I'd like to tell you a little anecdote. I was conducting a seminar of federal judges on jury trial, and we reached this issue of whether we were at the point of such complexity in science and technology that the jury system had broken down. During a break a seventy-year old federal judge from North Carolina told me this little story. He was trying a jury trial case in North Carolina—a six-person jury, which is now more common than the twelve-person jury. The issues in the case involved extraordinary technical questions about metallurgy and metal fatigue. A huge truck drive-train had gone haywire, and the claim was that it had been negligently manufactured. An enormous drive-train had been set up in the courtroom for the experts to testify about, and the experts went on for hours and hours and hours. The judge said to me: "Frankly, Arthur, I didn't know what the hell they were talking about! After we took a break and came back to the courtroom, there were the six jurors around the drive-train. They were assembling and disassembling it, with no supervision. So I called over the experts and I said, 'Do you know what the hell they're doing?' And the experts said, 'Judge, they're doing it absolutely perfectly!' That renewed my belief in juries." So who knows where intelligence begins and ends? And who knows what is beyond the compass of any human being?

CHAPTER 7

Strategic Planning
and
Computer Technology

Chapter 7A

Values, Technology, and Strategic Choice

*James Brian Quinn**

This paper will develop three central themes: (1) Computer-electronics technology is so powerful that the question is no longer "Can we do it?" but "What is the right thing to do?". (2) If we allow these choices to be made by "hidden hand" of traditional economics or the "authoritarian hand" of centrist philosophies, the results will be disastrous for mankind. New potentials call for new long-term strategies dictated by new visions and not by expediency or dogmas of the past. (3) Choices made will affect the destinies of entire nations, the relationships between nations, and the way nations govern themselves and interact with the world.

These choices are profoundly value and ethics laden. The balance of the goals society seeks and the means it uses to pursue them derive from and will affect its most deeply held philosophical and religious beliefs.[1] And these will be strategic choices in the truest meaning of that word. They will affect the direction entire cultures can take as well as the viability of those cultures in the future. Unfortunately one can only indicate and highlight some key trends and choices in a brief presentation.[2]

*Buchanan Professor of Management, Amos Tuck School of Business Administration, Dartmouth College

A MOST POWERFUL TECHNOLOGY

Computer electronics cannot be arbitrarily separated from such other important aspects of electronics as communications, power-servo-automation systems, and bioelectronics technologies. Computers are merely components or substitute systems in all of these. Computers switch, stack, control, and modulate communications for transmission and receiving devices. They instruct, guide, and provide memory for power-servo units. They operate mechanical limbs, artificial hearts, synthetic eyes, CAT scanners, life support systems, and so on. They control consumer devices, industrial processes, and modern weaponry. Electronics is perhaps the most powerful of all recent technologies in terms of its impact on our lives. It may be supplanted in this role by genetic engineering in the 1990s.[3] But electronics capabilities are nowhere near their probable ultimate limits. A few examples will suggest some awesome present capabilities and perhaps pose a glimmer of what is yet to come.

Growing Demand

Current estimates show that use of electronic functions has been growing exponentially for some time. (See Figure 1.) Demand has grown by some 2,000 times since the initial introduction of the integrated circuit in the early 1960s[4] and appears likely to grow by at least another 100 times during the next decade.

Since most studies to date indicate that some 75 to 80 percent of all major technological advances in this century have been demand driven,[5] further electronics innovations are likely in the foreseeable future. And diffusion theory suggests that advance rates will probably be exponential until theoretical limits are approached.[6] An almost endless demand for communication, calculation, automation, measurement, sensing, guidance, and control systems seems to ensure future research, development, and entrepreneurial risktaking for these technologies over any reasonable future horizon.

Switching Capabilities

The capabilities of the existing technology are already mind-boggling. To suggest some of its dimensions: let us consider the total information transferred by the interaction of the brains and optical cortices of all the human beings in the world.

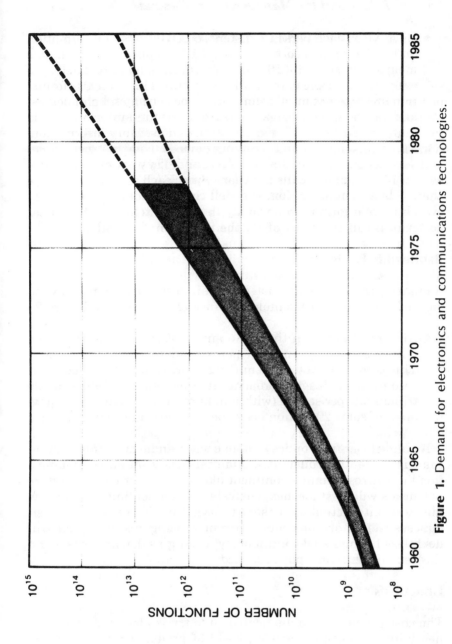

Figure 1. Demand for electronics and communications technologies.

- Each year, each person registers some 10^{18} bits of information on his/her optical cortex. With 4×10^9 people in the world, this means that some 4×10^{27} bits of information are received optically by all people in the world each year. This optical information swamps the aural information received by human beings, and can be used as some measure of the total information humans receive—minus general tactile and sensory information.

It is interesting that the Bell Telephone System can currently switch 10^{27} telephone calls per year.[7] Since each call involves more than 4 bits of information, the Bell System alone can currently switch more information annually than is switched by the optical cortex-brain interactions of all the people in the world.

Bandwidth Potentials

Similarly, the bandwidth potentials of lasers—as the next extension of transmission technologies—are enormous. (See Figure 2.)

- At current states of the art, a single laser can transmit some billion bits of information per second through fiber optics.[8] This is equivalent to transmitting approximately 200 books per second. If the laser approaches its theoretical potential of 100 trillion bits per second (within light frequency bands), an equivalent of some 20 million books per second could be transmitted.

A single laser-fiber-optics system could handle more information than is currently transmitted simultaneously by all communication links across a major continent like North America. Thus future potentials will exist for inexpensively communicating entirely new modes of intellectual or sensory information. The first light-fiber-optics systems are of course currently being installed and will doubtless be improved continuously as long as demand exists and theoretical limits are not broached.

Unit Costs

The cost per unit of sophisticated circuitry is also dropping exponentially. As usage increases, costs of production drop continuously—at a rate of approximately 28 percent for each doubling of production.[9] An initial intergrated chip configuration may still cost close to $100,000. But if one produces millions of the same chip, the cost drops asymptotically toward zero. (See Figure 3.)[10] The

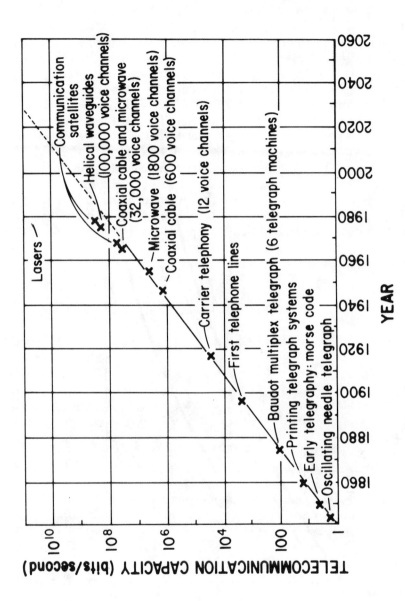

Figure 2. Sequence of inventions of telecommunications.

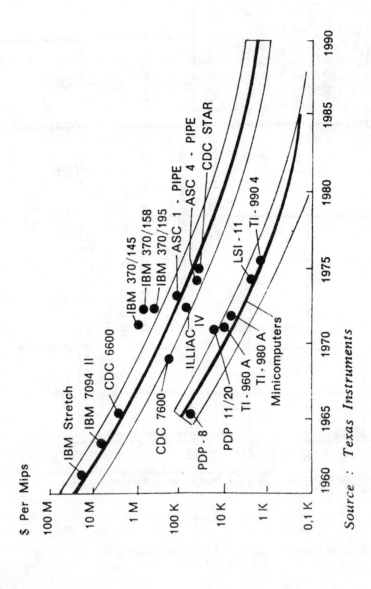

Figure 3. System cost per million instructions per second (maximum performance). (Courtesy of Texas Instruments)

result of this has been the rule of thumb in the computer industry that: "One can buy ten times the computing power each succeeding ten years for the same dollar amount" and that: "The marginal cost of the millionth good chip approaches 0."

Density of Information

Simultaneously the capacity to mount ever-increasing quantities of information on a single chip is growing exponentially. The number of active components an advanced integrated circuit can contain has been doubling almost annually for years. And the capacity of memory chips for computers and microcomputers has also been growing exponentially. (See Figure 4.) As a result, some of the most powerful central processors of the 1960s can now be packaged as "pocket" units. Memory storage that used to occupy complete rooms can now be contained in file-cabinet sized or smaller units.

- For example: Assuming that some 70 million different books (not including multiple copies of the same book) would approximate the aggregate of all individual and important books in the major libraries of the world, one could now store their contents on approximately 700 large movie reels of intensely developed microfilm or on some 7,000 holograms. Yet if one assumes that it will be ultimately possible to store a bit of information on an atom or molecule—not an unreasonable assumption given today's microchemistry—storage capacity is only limited by Avogadro's Number. Simple calculations indicate that all the bits of information in some 70 million books (10^{14} to 10^{15} bits) theoretically could be stored in a fraction of an atomic lattice one cubic centimeter in dimension.

All these examples merely illustrate that current computer-electronics technologies are extremely powerful. But theoretical limits have not yet been approached for most important aspects of these technologies. With miniaturization of component sizes limited only by electron-beam scribing capabilities or the capacity of atoms or molecules to hold bits of information, exponential progress on chip technology should continue for the foreseeable future. In fact, most experts state that no theoretical limits will prevent progress within the next decade. The biggest limitations are in accessing the chips and in input/output devices. And software development will also pose some potential limits. But these may be attacked by voice I/O systems and by machine programmable techniques. With such

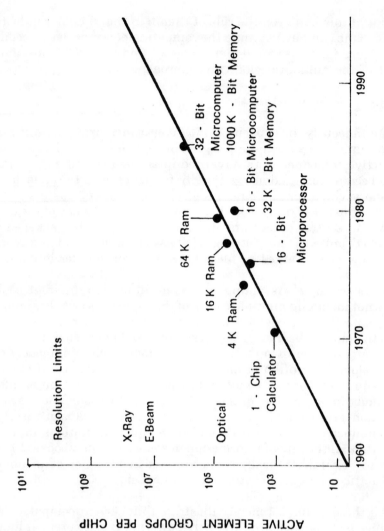

Figure 4. Semiconductor chip complexity. (Courtesy Texas Instruments)

124

capabilities, the issue is clearly not so much, "What can we do?" but "What should we do and with what priorities?". I will group my comments under three major headings: (1) basic values issues, (2) relationships among nations, and (3) the knowledge strategy.

BASIC VALUES ISSUES

As always, there are some perils associated with pursuing such wide-ranging advances. Some people have foreseen unemployment, thought control, centralization of society, conformity, invasion of privacy, dependency, the loss of freedom, and even the creation of subservient human androids as probable outgrowths of their use. Indeed these were the dominating themes of the post–World War II and 1960s literature.[11] Some earlier papers have suggested specific abuses and potentials for harm, and I will not develop these further here. But for the most part, prevailing ethics have led to other choices and to other results. What basic trends and values issues do they suggest for the future?

Opportunities and Freedom of Choice

Although there have been displacements of employment, virtually all major studies to date agree that automation has increased, rather than decreased, total jobs available.[12] As costs for an automated industry's goods drop, the goods are relatively more demanded, volume typically increases, and distribution and support systems expand to maintain them in the field. Entire older industries, such as buggy wheels, may be replaced. But new options and choices are created, and whole new industries arise. Figures 5 and 6 show quite clearly that without the development of the information industry and the service sector (dominantly arising from electronics, computer, and communications technologies) total employment would indeed have been a problem.

- For example: today's telephone, telegraph, television, radio, ocean shipping, navigation, aircraft, finance, insurance, banking, accounting, energy production, energy distribution, mass production, mass transportation, travel, sports, medical, life support, environmental control, and even government systems would be impossible without computer-electronics. Only shadows of their total current and future opportunities could exist.

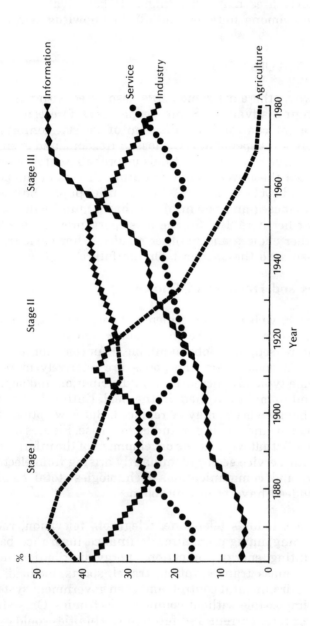

Figure 5. The four sectors of the U.S. labor force, by percent, 1860–1980 (using median estimates of information workers). (*Source:* Marc Porat, *The Information Economy: Definition and Measurement,* Office of Telecommunications Special Publication 77–12 (1), May 1977.

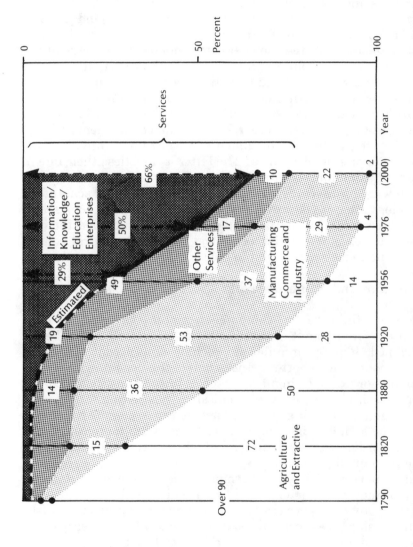

Figure 6. Post-industrial society workforce distribution: dominance of information/knowledge/education activities. (*Source:* G. T. Molitor, "The Path to Post Industrial Growth," *The Futurist,* April 1981, © PPFI 1980.)

And perhaps just as importantly, these technologies have been—and will continue to be—among the most prolific bases for new, small, decentralized enterprises. They have not just created the massive bureaucracies many fear. Hundreds of thousands of small businesses and service units have enhanced individuals' choices of services and life styles, decentralized the society, and enabled greater job choice in widely dispersed areas. Without such opportunities the ethic of free choice becomes hollow. Can one really be free, in the Western philosophical sense, without a right to choose among a variety of work alternatives, employers, and even the creative risks of starting one's own unique entity?

This is a basic value issue. Will computer-electronic technologies be allowed to create ever more free choices for employment and user benefits? Or will they be regulated and centralized into giant bureaucracies or state combines? The latter is doubtless their fate in advanced communist-centrist states. Elsewhere, after an early start toward large-scale national monopolies, the small scale of the technology seems to be prevailing. Deregulation of this sector seems to be the current mode in the United States. And many feel the very scale and flexibility of the technology will make central control and regulation elsewhere impossible.[13]

The Nature and Value of Work

In a more finite realm, computer-electronics technologies offer potentials for automating routine tasks on a scale never before envisioned. Reprogrammable microchips now permit automatic process control for short-run tasks where this was previously impossible—for example, in machine tool setups, typing, batch chemical processing, hard copy transmission, typesetting, and so on. Interestingly, surviving production tasks in automated factories tend to be simpler for shop workers rather than more complex.[14] Just as word processors allow a relatively new typist to produce the same high quality results only an experienced executive secretary could achieve in the past, automatic process controls frequently allow a quality of factory production which could previously be achieved only by superb craftsmen. Consequently production tasks can increasingly be decentralized to areas where less skilled workers live—virtually any place in the world—with fascinating potentials for wealth redistribution and greater workforce access for those with less training.

The most disagreeable tasks in production can often be automated—and are automated first—allowing remaining jobs to be more humane and flexible. This is the basic approach to automation in the U.S. and Swedish auto companies. In summary, automation, accompanied by appropriate full employment policies, can mean more and better jobs for the less skilled, as well as greater technical challenges for those who design, develop, and maintain the automated equipment. This has often been the pattern in the past.

Wealth Definition and Appreciation

But unfortunately when workers are able to produce so much more with so little effort, they tend to lose identity with their output.[15] There is less of the craftsman's sense of contribution. Many people therefore begin to deride the value of the output from work and the values of work itself.[16] Since production output seems so easily available, there is a pressure toward egalitarianism in its distribution—the "entitlement society". Attitudes develop that all should share equally regardless of their efforts. Consequently those less desirable remaining tasks which cannot be automated (currently street cleaning, sewer maintenance, crop picking, and so on) cannot attract the employment they need.

All this can lead either to breakdowns in social services, as it has in some central cities, or to a silent restructuring of incentive systems so that these "least desirable" jobs pay more than traditionally "sought-after" employment.

- In the latter case an interesting reordering of society's perceived values for various tasks tends to result, with manual jobs becoming more socially "acceptable" than they have been in recent years. It has now become almost fashionable for a college graduate to be a carpenter, or plumber, or farmer—jobs scorned in the recent past.

This same unparalleled capacity to increase output and create new options quickly begins to strain societies' traditional regard for wealth generation and its measurements of wealth itself. In the past most economies have measured efficiency and wealth production in terms of physical output per person. However, once a society's gross demands for food, shelter, health, and transportation are met—not too difficult in an advanced automated society like Sweden with a stable population base—any sensible measure of wealth must move into other realms where classical economic models break down. Measurable economic rationality—a most cherished value—quickly comes under assault.

- For example: Is a high-consumption society in a modern city-jungle wealthier than a comfortably self-sufficient rural community? Is a society belching smoke and litter, polluting its streams and aquifers, and destroying its resources and natural beauties richer than one that produces somewhat less physical output and fewer of these insults?

The extension of humanity's physical prowess through automation has made this a relevant question only in the last few years. And the choice of progress measures and strategies in response to these questions presents profound value issues that traditional economics handle very badly.

Great affluence combined with extensive communications technologies helps create the values of the "me" and "now" society and its concepts of goodness, benefit, or wealth.

- Given the emotional impact and urgency of electronic media, young people today quickly witness psychological traumas, science spectaculars, world events, assassinations, sports, art, and drama that few adults ever experienced in prior ages. In many respects these children are less naive, more informed, and more sanguine than any prior generation. But, like the soldiers of World War I, "it's hard to keep them down on the farm after they've seen Paris." Many are ready for thrills or risks their age groups never previously imagined.

Properly trained and challenged, this could be the most productive, exciting group of new citizens in history. But the group's values have been strongly shaped by the choices of thrill-laden programs and sense-centered advertising messages that bombarded their forming consciences. How much thought do programmers, copywriters, or networks give to the ultimate impact of their decisions?[17] And what can be done about this thoughtlessness?

In this environment many people are led to one escalating sensate thrill after another—not of course by the media alone. A market economist might argue that their actions were optimizing the values of their expenditures to themselves. Hence they pose no significant issues in terms of traditional economic values. But again, one must ask whether a society that has been taught to consume more in more nonnutritious foods, cosmetics, macho appliances, and drugs is truly wealthier than one that has lower measured output but has been taught to value better education, outdoor life, homes, personal safety, and so on. With the greater productivity of automation and the instant communication potentials of television, nations are forced into value choices in which traditional market mechanisms and wealth measurements often provide poor vehicles for strategic analysis or public choice. The wealthiest societies in the future will be those which cause their electronic capabilities to be applied to the highest and best use, not those who are the greatest producers and users of physical goods.

Traditional economic models, which dominate the measures used for policy purposes, significantly distort the analysis and predicted impact of strategic choices. As is well known, these models measure the output value of many service or public use sectors on the basis of input cost. This leads to peculiar results.

- For example, if better electronic sensors, monitors, and control systems produce clean rivers at lower cost, total output (as now measured) seems to drop. And if the cleaner river also improves human health, demand for health services will drop with a further negative impact on Gross National Product. Similarly, a longer-lasting, gas-conserving, computer-monitored automobile sold at the same price as a fast-decaying dinosaur will lower total auto and service production and negatively affect GNP for automotive, distribution, services, and energy sectors.

Such distortions may not be as significant when basic consumption needs are unsatisfied, but they are positively misleading to policy in an affluent society.

What is needed is a shift from "output-per-person" measures to "values-produced-per-person" measures. To accomplish this, new sets of social indicators must replace traditional economic measures and obtain equal acceptability in policy decisions. These must value public consumption and public markets fairly against private consumption at the margin. Simply stated, a clean river is equally as valuable an output and as valid a market for goods and services as some number of snowmobiles.[18] But current economic measures and attitudes do not treat them the same way. New intellectual and analytical constructs are needed that approach public demands as worthwhile growth markets for a decentralized society, not just as punitive costs to be assessed against a few.[19] Such changes require academic and public leadership that has been notably lacking.

Concepts of Democracy

Electronic communications have begun to reshape the very form and nature of political processes. The bombardment of four to six hours per day of television significantly affects both childrens' and adults' perceptions of reality. With only a few hundred people dominating the choice of material shown during prime hours, we have a new power elite—elected by no one, but with a continuous forum for presenting their ideas in a fashion few leaders in history have enjoyed.

- For example, TV media personalities can essentially substitute their views for those of elected officials or make such officials ineffectual in carrying out a desired policy. Immediately after the President completes a major speech, the media give at least equal time to reporters, opponents, and noninformed "man in the street" surveys. This allows people who have less knowledge and no specific responsibility to pick at parts of the total policy—with no obligation for enunciating another policy that deals with all the subtleties the President had so carefully to consider.

At best, this process fragments policymaking, creating what appears to be a unified opposition where there was none. For example, when the governors of Michigan, California, Colorado, and Louisiana commented negatively on Carter's energy policy, they appeared to represent a coalition against this policy, although their separate goals were often more severely in conflict than their differences with Carter. In extreme circumstances, media coverage can escalate a particular policy choice out of proportion or decrease policy options disastrously for a chief executive.

- Clear examples exist in the Iranian hostage situation, recent hijackings, and now prevalent attempts of the media to "get more action coverage" in an El Salvador war the Administration wishes it could quietly end.

New mechanisms are needed at national and network policy levels to ameliorate the effects these market-driven choices may have on world events. The leverage the technology allows is too great to avoid such considerations.

Consensus Processes

Communications technologies are also reshaping traditional consensus processes. They allow single-issue constituencies to obtain exposure, thus escalating otherwise minor issues into major political focal points. This further fragments political processes, making it difficult for a political figure to achieve broad unifying consensus. Effective video presentations often offer vignettes and simplify positions for dramatic impact, making more moderate consensus opinions hard to maintain in complex situations. Electronic media also tend to overemphasize the visual image versus the capabilities or arguments of individual proponents, promoting appearance, emotionalism, and theatrical skills to new highs in politics. This effect may be further compounded as television enters the courtroom in tests of laws that require subtlety in interpretation.

Electronics media have changed basic relationships between the politician and his constituency. The political policymaker must be ready to respond instantly to high-amplitude verbal attacks and bizarre political demonstrations transmitted from anywhere in the world, knowing these have entered his constituents' homes with a seemingly strident imperative for action. These incursions make it much more difficult to resolve issues through compromise in a quiet atmosphere of negotiation. These extensive potentials for fragmentation, demagoguery, and harassment have placed great pressures on one of democracy's strongest implicit values—rule through consensus and compromise. To deal with these pressures, governments have often attempted control of the media, with the inherent dangers of that policy. Short of this extreme, dealing with media issues has become at least as important in policy formulation as the substantive questions themselves.

Referendum Democracy

In a conference like this we tend to dwell on negative aspects that require policy solutions. But we must not forget that inexpensive communication technologies could soon make referendum democracy more feasible, perhaps coping with some of the very issues the technology has raised for policymakers.

- As every home has an inexpensive video display unit and a computer transponder, it will become possible to have direct popular votes on important issues, potentially leading to increased social decentralization, local identity, and local responsibility. When communications and social infrastructures permit (as in small towns in New England or in Switzerland) referendum democracy seems likely to develop.

But then policymakers will encounter a new problem—properly informing populations on crucial issues. How cable TV systems are conceived, financed, licensed, and installed will have great impact on how these systems are used for such democratizing purposes, as well as for banking, shopping, health, security, entertainment, and government services in the future. Unfortunately there is little evidence that current planning will use their full potentials. How does one factor such high-level value choices as referendum democracy into the institutions which manage cable television?

INTERNATIONAL STRATEGIC ISSUES

Electronics technologies will doubtless continue to change relationships between sovereign nations. Increasingly products can be produced anywhere in the world because of the capacity to automate processes, achieve international quality standards, and communicate with parent, coordinating, or marketing organizations in other countries. This can lead to true internationalization of production—by multinational corporations or simply through extended trade relationships. Electronics technologies help train host country work and maintenance forces, link host countries with market countries, and internationalize finance and risk for smaller countries. Along with internationalization of production and markets comes integration of interests among sovereign nations and a potential decline of nationalism versus internationalism in outlook. Given the massive scale of the worldwide investments needed to develop and deliver food, energy, and mineral resources in the late 1900s, these technologies provide an important supporting force favoring wealth redistribution, trade stabilization, and new international coalitions in future decades.

New Cultural Patterns

The implications for developing countries could be dramatic. Electronic technologies allow the time for training and dissemination of skills to be significantly foreshortened and productivity to be quickly enhanced. But automation-communications technologies also embody the knowledge and values of other cultures. This—

and the discipline industrial production demands—tends to stimulate in many cultures patterns identified with "advanced nations." This is especially true as production reaches levels that permit mass distribution, automotive transportation, and some increased discretionary consumption. Unfortunately rich local cultural differences tend to be submerged as a "Westernization" process sets in. Black suits, glass buildings, and supermarkets soon replace much more colorful and personal local institutions.

Once in place, large-scale communications systems tend to approach "zero marginal cost" for each additional message. This includes the satellite systems linking countries together. Thus communications with outside groups can rapidly proliferate. Given the low cost, high power, and great flexibility of modern communications technologies, it becomes extremely difficult for host countries to screen out "hostile ideas."

- As people become aware of the "better life" or "greater freedom" of other countries, they are likely to question highly authoritarian structures, prevailing religious myths, or arbitrary class segmentations in their own society. The attitude becomes: "Others have goods and freedom, why don't we? They don't get struck down by the old gods, why should we?"

Countries that rely on highly authoritarian governments, royal sovereigns, or rich aristocracies with extremely poor majority populations to provide their energy or mineral resources are likely to suffer severely. Yet this realization does not seem to have affected U.S. policy to date. If it doesn't soon, the country will pay a high price.

New Coalitions

On the other hand, with advanced automation and communications technologies come some fascinating possibilities. The standards implicit in those technologies form linkages that inevitably tie participants together in closer coalitions.

- For example, a regional satellite system or television system will cause the area to develop its industry around the standards, parts, and support capabilities that system demands. This creates long-term linkages among whole areas of the world. And these linkages can be strategically influenced if proper decisions are made now.

Hopefully new communications technologies will portend important strategic realignments in international relationships with: fewer distinct, xenophobic cultures, increased internationalism, and a much more highly integrated world more dependent on trade than ever before. But this requires a guiding national strategy and supporting corporate decisions to make the concept emerge.

Perhaps the most important long run impact of these new technologies will lie in: (1) how we deploy them for joint international development and (2) how we employ them for large-scale public decision purposes. Neither of these will evolve in proper directions without strategic thought and effort. Individuals, corporations, and political leaders must consciously stimulate national policies toward strategic—not expedient—ends.

- For example, some of the major facets of the new trade relationships with the People's Republic of China are those involving management technique and technology transfers to China. The resulting coalition between the U.S. and the People's Republic of China could perhaps be the most important single strategic development of the 1970s. Similar information-based strategies, coalitions, and countercoalitions are reshaping other national relationships worldwide. European-wide sharing of information, research programs, and production risks (in aircraft, computers, nuclear power) represent a coalition response to the penetration of large advanced U.S. technology companies. And one may soon see the U.S. government allow company coalitions to struggle against the Japanese challenge in world markets.

KNOWLEDGE AS A STRATEGY

Electronics technologies allow knowledge generation and dissemination to become a central feature of strategy for both private enterprises and governments.

- Very large international enterprises can only exist if they provide a value to host and parent countries which cannot be more effectively provided by other means. Essentially, large multinational companies in the future will transfer technology, capital or market access, and management skills in one direction in return for human energies, raw materials, and manufactured goods shipped in the other. Key elements in transnational companies' strategies increasingly are becoming: control over their technologies, their information access, their management skills, and the dissemination of these to their participating countries.

When properly used, computer-electronics-communications technologies can allow companies—and governments—to operate in a highly decentralized mode, with full confidence that their decentralized units are responding to desired goals and not wasting resources or undertaking disastrous risks. It has become possible to monitor not just production and financial information, but also performance in: pollution control, quality of output, technological advances, personnel development, and so forth at headquarters. This can allow large enterprises either to thoroughly decentralize organizations or to centralize them beyond all previous limits. Unfortunately too many larger organizations seem to use the technology for greater centralization. Believing they can exert centralized control, governments especially tend to centralize communications and information storage, often giving unelected bureaucrats power their populations never intended to relinquish. Thus the technology can, unless carefully planned, unwittingly change key relationships between individuals and the institutions dominating their lives. Positive strategies are needed in all large institutions to avoid such unintended consequences and to deal with the perceived threats and alienation large-size organizations tend to engender. Unfortunately most large enterprises and government units fail to realize that their policies of growth *à outrance* carry with them the threats of their own destruction. Nothing is strategically less viable than the unlimited institutional growth electronics could allow.

The Education-Information Society

As production becomes increasingly dispersed throughout the world, industrialized countries must arrive at new overall trade strategies. It will become even more difficult to export traditional mass-produced products in competition with low-cost developing country factories. For this reason various industrialized countries have focused on the "intelligence" industries as their basis for world trade. Highest value added per person tends to lie in creative and intelligent use of high technology products and concepts. Developing these systematically for export requires a positive national strategy explicitly imbedded in each nation's educational and research infrastructure.

Formal Education

Information technologies are already beginning substantially to redefine the entire nature, role, and methodologies of formal education. Both subject content and values tend increasingly to be learned from electronic devices. And in many respects these devices can be more effective than a teacher in a classroom. Computerized instruction for slow learners can actually give more individual attention than a teacher could. Technical subjects requiring substantial illustrative material may also be more easily and effectively taught from video. The "NOVA" science programs provide a formidable example. Where video communications are widespread, students at any educational level already tend to have a higher level of cognitive (or content) knowledge on many complex subjects than their peers had in earlier years.

The school's task therefore will probably change in significant ways. Less time will probably be needed for skills (like arithmetic), once learned through drills. These can be taught from programmed sources and practiced through devices like hand calculators and electronic games. The same is probably true for other cognitive skills as inexpensive programmed learning devices proliferate. Interestingly programmed devices have often been found to be more effective in teaching cognitive skills to slow or "differential" learners. Instead of receiving trenchant reinforcement of their "stupidity" from teachers and peers, slow learners can get constant positive reinforcement from programmed learning and proceed at their own pace, often quickly surpassing their performance in more socialized situations. And such self-taught skills may cause more permanent learning than the "rote skills" encouraged in many classrooms. But because children will tend to spend much more time with passive video entertainment and with nonhuman electronic learning devices, the school must take on more of a training role for social skills—and often for physical skills.

Because of significantly higher access to information through inexpensive communications, entire populations can quickly become much more aware, informed, and "intelligent" in the academic sense. People in the street can discuss issues only the literate elite could have encountered in the past. Communications technologies also expand libraries into "information centers" with access to worldwide and specialized information bases never previously conceived, thus extending the horizons of the intelligentsia as well. However, such technologies simultaneously make education much more *capital* intensive. While electronic devices increase the initial cost of the education system, they extend the reach of the few highly trained and skilled teachers. But they also make obsolete many traditional teaching concepts. Although traditional systems may yield grudgingly, communications technologies should offer developing areas with large capital resources a chance to rapidly educate their populations to very high levels, if they can properly adapt their education systems.

New Research Concepts

In order to support an "intelligence industry" strategy, research, development, and scientific/technical training must also be reemphasized in the society. Recognizing this fact, Japan, Germany, France, and Russia (among others) are already force feeding their engineering-technical schools and research institutions, while the United States has steadily fallen behind in its relative investments in both areas. This country badly needs consciously to reverse the "technological alienation" trend of the last decade if it expects to reestablish its formerly preeminent wealth-generating capabilities for the future.

Fortunately there are important pending breakthroughs and technological leads that justify supporting a stronger technical endeavor. Electronics technologies are ready for major advances in such areas as: information storage and playback (optical disc) technologies, laser-fiber optics, scanning-beam transmission technologies, data-compression technologies, electronic-mail capabilities, LADAR and LIDAR pollution analyses, voice input-output techniques, computer-assisted software development, translators, medical diagnostic and care techniques, life maintenance systems, and so on. Energy (notably fusion power, solar devices, and direct energy conversion techniques), agriculture (soil protection, pest control, genetically designed plants, and biological fertilization technologies) genetic-engineering, human health maintenance, ecological systems research, and so forth also offer burgeoning fields for productive research.

These potentials are supported by the capacity to convert libraries into "information centers" with worldwide access to data bases and specialized information sets. These have the potential of extending the horizons of intelligence beyond all previous capabilities. Dr. Lederberg has recently stated that within approximately a decade, automated search processes could "move from information retrieval to knowledge retrieval." Information systems should be able to generate and test hypotheses within themselves, without having arbitrary limits imposed by the imaginations of researchers. This may change the very nature of the research process, as well as its sometimes lagging productivity. Such techniques are in their early developmental stages in fields like epidemiology today. And they are ready to expand to other realms. Again this challenges a deeply held value that only humans can create and that such creation is the highest measure of human aspiration. Who is the new elite in these circumstances?

CONCLUSIONS

The impact of such potentials is mind-boggling in itself. To avoid a knowledge strategy through fear would be tragic. The country can no longer afford not to have such a strategy. A single breakthrough (such as controlled fusion, bioseparation of hydrogen from water in the presence of sunlight, or interferon-induced immunity to viruses) could pay marginal education and research costs in perpetuity. Major advances could easily achieve balance-of-payments savings which alone could completely fund any social or educational programs the most dedicated person would wish for. The potentials are boundless and exciting. The real question is whether we will respond strategically or allow our past institutions, allocation mechanisms, and short-term horizons to dominate and suboptimize our lives.

NOTES

1. See W. Guth and R. Tagiuri, "Personal Values and Corporate Strategy," *Harvard Business Review* (Sept.–Oct. 1965) for relations between values and strategic decisions.
2. Central concepts of strategy as used here are explained in R. Vancil and P. Lorange, *Strategic Planning System* (Englewood Cliffs, N.J.: Prentice-Hall, 1978), and K. Andrews, *The Concept of Strategy* (Homewood, Ill.: Richard D. Irwin, 1971).
3. "Genetic Engineering, Human Genetics, and Cell Biology," *Report of Subcommittee on Science, Research and Technology*, U.S. House of Representatives, August 1980.
4. R. Noyce, "Microelectronics," *Scientific American* (September 1977).
5. See especially J. Schmookler, *Innovation and Economic Growth* (Cambridge, Mass.: Harvard University Press, 1966), and J. Jewkes, D. Sawers, et al., *The Sources of Invention* (New York: St. Martins Press, 1958).

6. See R. Lenz, "Forecasts of Exploding Technology by Trend Extrapolation," in J. Bright (ed.), *Technological Forecasting for Industry and Government* (Englewood Cliffs, N.J.: Prentice-Hall, 1968).
7. L. Branscombe, "Information: The Ultimate Frontier," *Science* (12 Jan. 1979).
8. Ibid.
9. Noyce, "Microelectronics."
10. J. McHale, *World Facts and Trends* (New York: Macmillan, 1972).
11. D. Michaels, *Cybernation: The Silent Conquest* (Santa Barbara, Calif.: Center for Study of Democratic Institutions) was among the best known and quoted of this genre.
12. R. M. Solow, *Growth Theory an Exposition* (Oxford, England: Oxford University Press, 1970), and R. A. Solo and E. M. Rogers, *Inducing Technological Change for Economic Growth and Development* (East Lansing: Michigan State University Press, 1972) suggest some measures of the impact of such technologies on growth.
13. I. deSola Pool, "Technology Change and Modern Communications," *Technology Review* (Dec. 1980).
14. J. Bright, *Automation and Management* (Cambridge, Mass.: Harvard University Press, 1958). This is partially why unions oppose such technologies so strongly. Their members lose a skill monopoly even if more jobs are formed.
15. A. Toffler, *Future Shock* (New York: Bantam, 1971), develops this idea at some length.
16. H. Kahn and A. Wiener, *The Year 2000: A Framework for Speculation,* provided perhaps the first statement about the creation of a "neo sensati culture."
17. For example, in April 1981 The Media Institute of Washington, D.C., released an interesting study, *Crooks, Conmen, and Clowns,* that analyzed the consistent antibusiness bias in the portrayal of executives on television programs.
18. J. K. Galbraith, author of *The Affluent Society* (1958), is probably the most articulate economic spokesman of the tradeoffs between public needs and private consumption.
19. In J. B. Quinn, "Public Markets: Growth Opportunities and Environmental Improvement," *Technology Review* (June 1974), and in "The Next Big Market: Environmental Improvement," *Harvard Business Review* (September–October 1971), I try to provide a framework for this approach.

Computers and Business Strategy

Sidney Schoeffler*

Let me describe briefly what The Strategic Planning Institute does because I will be addressing myself to the issues of this conference against that backdrop. We assemble rather detailed information on the activities and performance levels of a group of individual businesses. The information is contributed by about 250 corporations, mostly in North America, but drawn increasingly from the rest of the world. The units of reporting on these corporations are the individual product businesses, what are increasingly coming to be called the "strategic business units."

The kind of information reported by each of these businesses includes such particulars as answers to the following questions: First, what kinds of *actions* have you been taking in your business? For example, what have you been *doing* about pricing, about capacity expansion, about personnel policy, about marketing programs, about new product introductions, about inventories, about accounting systems, and so forth? Second, what kind of *market* were you attempting to reach? Was it a growing or nongrowing market, stable or unstable, local, national, or international? Third, what kind of *competition* did the business have to contend against in attempting to serve that market? Were there many competitors, few competitors, large competitors, small competitors, nice competitors, ugly competitors? Fourth, what *results* have you been

*The Strategic Planning Institute

getting from taking those actions, in that market, against those competitors? What, in fact, happened to profits, to cash flow, to market share, to growth, and so forth? All of this information flows then into the data base, and the mission of our organization is to carry out two associated programs revolving around this data base. First, there is a *research* program, which identifies the underlying regularities visible in all this information: the laws of the market-place—the empirical regularities in the way that competitive markets behave that determine what moves under what conditions produce what kind of results. The findings of that research are then incorporated into a series of models; and these models, in turn, are used as *tools of planning* by the participating organizations.

Our program involves the kind of technology that is the subject of this conference at two levels. At the first level it is highly computerized; without that, the approach would have been totally impossible. Both the data collection and the very extensive "data crunching" required to gain insight from the information we receive must be computerized. Second, there is a rather new technology of statistical economic research employed with this technology of information handling and "number crunching"; we are merging these two technologies.

We are merging them, of course, because we think it is a good idea. I certainly realize that ours is not the only possible point of view. Because business corporations also have rights of privacy, and because their rights or privacy are rather closely associated with the rights of privacy of individual human beings, the merged technology might, somewhere down the line, create a problem. But I don't think this necessarily needs to happen. There are rather simple ways of avoiding such problems. (As a matter of fact, I think we *are* avoiding the likelihood that, somewhere down the line, this technology will become an instrument of economic or political dictatorship.) Let me explain some of the reasons why I think that our approach is, in the final analysis, a good idea. My argument is based on three propositions.

Proposition 1: You cannot act "ethically" or "morally" if you are oblivious to the consequences of your actions. There are some principles of ethics and morality that apply to the *act itself* (such as "thou shalt not kill"), and these principles are of course important for the way in which society needs to function. But in many cases the "goodness" or "badness" of an action resides almost entirely in the consequences that it produces. Most of the courses of action not treated in the Ten Commandments or in the Golden Rule are, insofar as the actions themselves are concerned, ethically *neutral.* That certainly is true for most economic actions. Therefore, if you want to be a high-minded, wonderful human being, what you usually have to do is to estimate the consequences of your actions. If the consequences promise to be good, then you are a good guy; and if the consequences promise to be bad, then you are a bad guy.

Proposition 2: You cannot predict the consequences of your actions in a complex or moderately complex social system if you do not know the "laws of nature" which govern that social system. Given this situation, what you must engage in is *science* because acquiring the ability to predict is impossible without it. The ability to predict any phenomenon is based on empirically observed regularities of nature; and science is the discipline that allows you to (a) derive the regularities which (b) you can then use to predict the consequences of your actions, which (c) then permits you to determine whether you're being a good guy or a bad guy.

Proposition 3: Science is intrinsically cross-sectional. The only way you can ever learn anything about your own situation is by comparing it in some disciplined way with *other* situations that bear certain structural similarities to yours. For example, consider the way in which human beings are studied by the medical sciences. (I cite the medical sciences as an illustration of applying scientific procedures to human problems because most people consider them to be "good" rather than "bad.") Suppose you are in a strange city, and you get chest pains; you go to a physician who looks at you and says, "take three of these pink pills and tomorrow you'll feel better." How does the physician make the forecast that allows the prescription of these three pink pills? The physician (or some supporting research organization) had, prior to your having presented this problem, looked at *other* people who had chest pains. Some of these other people who had chest pains looked like you— they were roughly the same age, the same body build, the same sex, the same weight, had the same cholesterol count, and had other similar characteristics. The investigation of these other people had tested various treatments of your symptoms, including those three pink pills. When the doctor confidently estimates that if *you* take those pink pills tomorrow *you* will feel better, that confidence comes from the fact that when the *other people like you* had those same symptoms, and when *they* took those pink pills, *they* felt better. Sometimes the physician understands *why* the desired result occurs and sometimes not. We still don't know how aspirin works; the important thing is to know that it *does* work in a sufficiently predictable way that the forecast of consequences can be made with reasonable confidence (at least to the point where you are much better off *using* that forecast than *rejecting* it).

All other applied sciences are intrinsically cross-sectional in the same sense. The way you know that a certain bridge you are thinking of building is going to stand up is that *other* bridges designed in this same way and placed in a comparable location have stood up. The only way you know that a certain type of seed and a certain type of fertilizer will work on your farm is because that type of seed and that type of fertilizer worked in other farms under comparable environmental conditions.

My next point: Cross-sectional research, which leads to science, which leads, in turn, to the predictability enabling you to estimate the consequences of your actions and choose "good" actions, *requires data bases.* You cannot do cross-sectional research without data bases. You need a medical data base to find out what epidemiological approaches work; you need nutritional data bases to find out what vitamins work; you need kidney treatment data bases to find out what kidney treatments work; and you need agricultural data bases to find out what fertilizers work. It is therefore necessary to collect *standardized* information from a variety of sources to be able to achieve whatever benefit there may be in science. This applies in medicine, in agriculture, in engineering, and it also applies in business. The only way in which the economy can be made to work better, other than by employing better physical technologies, is by being able to draw on better data bases. We need good technology for making business decisions. Very large economic resources are dissipated by people making erroneous economic decisions. Decisions that allocate resources to (a) businesses, (b) courses of action, and (c) individual products often turn out to waste these resources because there isn't an adequate demand for them, or because that demand does not occur in the expected place or at the expected time. Let me elaborate on this point by referring back to Arthur Miller's dramatic talk. He identified some of the misuses of the mountains of statistics being assembled about human beings. But he may have chosen a bad example in describing the screening procedure for law school applications as a horrible instance of abuse. Although I am not familiar with how schools screen their applications for admission, if a good scientific approach *preceded* the calculation of the number "1400" as an index predicting success in law school or in law, then there is nothing intrinsically wrong with using the index as a tool. If the number "1400" was, however, just some bureaucratic drone's opinion, then of course it would be worthless and mischievous. But if there were a real study done to determine what kinds of people turn out to be effective and successful lawyers, and if this research were adequately represented in the scoring system, then the scoring system may well be a noble thing, because it would help prevent the waste of lives and human resources that would occur if people who would make bad lawyers went to law school. And it is of general benefit to society that the lawyers who do graduate from law school turn out to be effective rather than ineffective.

At SPI, the way we try to keep our economic information from being misused (by the Justice Department or anyone else) is by a series of procedures that safeguard the privacy of that information. Let me describe what these procedures are. First, when a company puts information into our data base, we ask that company *not to identify* their business. We could feel comfortable about the non-identification because prior research carried out by the General Electric Company, where the identity of the businesses *was* known, disclosed that the identity of a business is not relevant to understanding its behavior. In the medical analogy that I've mentioned, when certain people with certain problems were given certain pills, we didn't need to know *who* the people were. We didn't need to know their names, religion, or political beliefs. All we needed to know was their weight, age, height, sex, cholesterol count, and other impersonal information. In this process do we lose the "humanity" of the individuals that we are looking at? Yes, we do. But that's the aim. We actually don't want to know more about them than we need to know, not only because that might be an invasion of their privacy but also because it would certainly increase the cost of the study. The same is true in the area of business. Therefore we ask companies that participate in the data base to not tell us what their business is, but just to describe it in terms of the abstract characteristics that are relevant to the purpose.

Second, we ask the companies to further disguise their businesses by concealing their magnitude so that no inference can be drawn from magnitude to identity. We ask the companies to multiply all of their numerical data by an arbitrary constant. They can do this without distorting the ratios or the trends in the data; and it is ratios and trends that are the critical characteristics of the business. By the time a business is recorded in this way, even if unauthorized people were to get hold of the information (in or outside a tyranically minded government), all they will discover are some characteristics of an unidentifiable business.

A final point: Suppose the universal data base on human beings that Arthur Miller was so rightly worried about were, in fact, to come into being. He was certainly right on the possible misuses; but let us look a little further at the possible benefits. Just as we at SPI, with our rather small data base, are able to give businesses some fairly good advice as to how they should conduct themselves, a national data base could make it possible to give to the individuals recorded in it some pretty good advice about how they should conduct their affairs. This advice should, in turn, enable them to lead more productive, more satisfying, and healthier lives. To give you an idea of how this might work, let me describe briefly what analyses are being done on the businesses in our data base. I am not claiming that we know the "right" way to do it; but our experience will provide an insight as to what might be possible at the level of individuals.

Suppose you are a company and your business is recorded in our data base in our standardized format. The variables that we ask people to report include simple market share, relative market share, degree of capital intensity, degree of vertical integration, degree of product superiority or inferiority, degree of labor productivity, degree of capital productivity, and growth rates of the served market. Why these characteristics? Because they are the most relevant for expressing the "laws of nature" required to predict the consequences of current business actions. Suppose then that your business is recorded in the data base in terms of those characteristics. We have a computer program that then performs the following steps: It searches the rest of the data base for other businesses that are similar to yours—strategic "look-alikes." This does not mean that they manufacture the same product (the identity of the product doesn't matter), but that they are look-alikes in terms of their important business characteristics: similar market share, similar relative market share, similar growth rates, similar capital intensity, similar R&D efforts, similar marketing efforts. Having found these look-alikes, the program subdivides them into two categories: those businesses that started out in the same position you are in now and went on to become "winners," and those businesses that began in a strategically comparable position but became "losers." (You, the user, can define "winning" and "losing" in any way you like. You can define "winning," for example, as being profitable, or as having positive cash flow, or as experiencing growth of employees, and so on.) After you have defined "winning," the computer program uses that definition to find the winners and the losers among the strategic look-alikes, and carries out a rather detailed examination of the behavior patterns of both "winners" and "losers." It determines what they did about their pricing, marketing, personnel, inventories, and so on, for the purpose of discovering differences. After finding areas of behavior in which the behavior of the winners differs from that of the losers, it performs a test of the statistical significance of that difference. (I hope you know that until you make such a test, you never know what you have found. Differences that are not statistically significant are irrelevant.) Typically the program discovers between five and fifteen behavior differences that effectively differentiate the winners from the losers in a statistically significant way. These behavior differences imply a course of action for your business, which, if you were to take it, would probably set you on the same trajectory as that of the winners, and point you away from the trajectory of the losers.

Ours is a standard program that happens to be running now in the area of business strategic planning. But it could operate on other data bases as well. Suppose we had the kind of national data base that Arthur Miller is nervous about, and suppose that your behavior, your medical characteristics, and so on, were all recorded there. How could we make benign use of it? Each of us should be able to search this data base for other people who, at one point in their lives, were in the same position as we are in now. We could then use our own personal definitions of "winning" to examine what kinds of educational programs, medical treatment, geographic location, and human associations would set us on the course of the winners, and would minimize the chance of taking the course of the losers.

I think we would all then be able to govern our lives not only in a more ethical way, but also in a more productive and happier way. Are there some risks in this? Yes, there are. There always are; but with adequate attention to these risks, there is probably a technically feasible way of reducing them to an acceptable level, while preserving many of the benefits.

Discussion

Question: Let me join the last issue raised concerning a national data base and suggest why it might, in fact, be so terrible—terrible in a way that is different from the privacy issues addressed earlier by Arthur Miller and, to some extent, by Sid Schoeffler.

The problem is the spectre of a data base, and I'm not now worried about information getting into the wrong hands. I'm talking about something entirely different—the spectre of a data base that contains a sufficient amount of data about us as individuals so that the consequences of various choices can be accurately predicted or inferred statistically, thereby giving us advice as to what to do. This is scarier and, in fact, potentially more terrible and more dangerous, than some of the privacy invasions we've been talking about, but for a different reason. Let me see if I can explain it.

The extension from how this process works in businesses, where things are relatively easily quantifiable, to how it might work in our own lives, where things are highly qualitative, leads me to believe there would be great pressure to quantify things that are difficult to quantify. And I'll use as an example of that the very same attack that Arthur Miller made on the use of the board scores.

Clearly many of the qualities of the applicant simply do not get into that scoring/screening formula, and it is not a question of whether the right coefficients have been found. Many qualities are unquantifiable by nature, such as the amount of intellectual curiosity—the spark—and many of the things that do, in fact, have a great effect on success in school or in a career, but which escape that numerical equation. So many factors are left out. And I would be so much afraid that similar kinds of factors would be left out in the hypothetical proposal you suggest that, it seems to me, it would be taking away exactly those qualities of the human life which are not quantifiable.

Schoeffler: If what you say were true, that there are certain aspects of the human personality that are forever irreducible to data, then you would have the right concern. But I don't think it is true. I think all you have a right to say right now is that we don't know yet how some of these very important characteristics can be reduced to data.

Question: Let me modify my objection. What you say is very valid, I accept that. I'm basically a reductionist at heart myself. But in the same way that I sometimes have objections to some of the goals of artificial intelligence, I have to ask this question: Is the ultimate reduction to quantified returns, even if theoretically possible, desirable?

Schoeffler: We'll never know. We have to proceed on some element of faith. So far, in the area of human endeavor in which the element of science has ever been introduced, it has been irreversible; people never elected to go back to the former way of doing things. And this ought to give us some faith that if we were to introduce the element of data and science and rigorous analysis in the area of human qualities as well, that people, having seen how it works, would also not elect to go back to a former state.

Now as to your previous point with which I want to agree: Might incompetence, getting hold of the system, do terrible damage? Yes, it might. And that certainly is a risk.

Quinn: Let me point out a lesson of Love Canal. We cannot learn from Love Canal as yet, because we don't really know yet what happened there. We are unable to figure out where all the people are who might have been affected, and we don't know what has happened to them as individuals. If an adequate data base existed, we could not only identify what had happened to them, but we could identify other potential Love Canals. We could then save dozens of years in taking actions which affect human lives.

Again, I grant there are some dangers to this. But the benefits of being able to make certain types of analyses have enormous human value. And these deal with individuals and benefit individuals. And I think we must not lose sight of those in the fear that we have about the potential abuses of data bases.

Question: Why should corporate operations have the right to privacy?

Schoeffler: I don't have good data on that, but the common belief is that there is an association between economic freedom and political freedom—only that. To the extent that we do have data, the way in which the Nazis took over in Germany was to regulate the companies first and individual lives later.

And most of the fears that people have of the misuse of socialism in the socialist economies is that economic power leads to political power. Therefore, protection of economic privacy—and this is a bit of a leap—might be a guarantee of the protection of political privacy and other privacies. But I didn't mean necessarily to advocate that point of view.

Companies do have privacy right now. There are limits, shrinking limits, but these are limits beyond which the regulations cannot and probably should not go. And this is probably one reason why those companies that have chosen to participate in the program with us are relaxed about doing on a voluntary basis what they fight to the death if a political agency were to do it. And properly so.

Quinn: May I take a shot at that one also? When you use the word "company," what do you mean? I'm an individual; I have a company which is my own. Am I to be intruded upon by anyone because of that? Jerry and I join together in a project; we form a company for that purpose. Are we to be intruded upon because of that act?

At what stage, then, do you break into that chain of individuals who can associate in certain ways? That's where I think the real ethical problem lies. And I think we've tried as a society to find rules of that intervention which are acceptable to both parties.

Just for background information, the concept of privacy, as it developed in American law, has not included business organizations. The Privacy Act of 1974, for example, that Arthur Miller spoke about this morning, only covers individuals, human individuals, not legal persons like corporations. There are other kinds of privacy which don't usually get the name privacy, such as trade secrets and similar things. So we do have areas where there's protection, and regulation limits also. But we haven't in this country called in privacy. Now in many European countries, they do call it privacy. And many of the European privacy statutes—data protection statutes—lump human beings together with legal persons for protecting privacy. That's not what we have done in our legal tradition.

CHAPTER 8

Computers:
Fast Instruments and
Slow Minds

*Clarence C. Walton**

Certain revolutions hit society soundlessly—frogs' feet landing on concrete walks. No blood is spilled, no buildings destroyed, no armies routed, no heroes honored. Often there is little public awareness of their coming, the significance of their presence, or the reach of their ultimate consequence. Yet when such silent revolutions appear, no informed individual doubts that civilization is being irreversibly transformed, that massive new problems are being created, and that necessary and appropriate solutions will come haltingly.

Such a revolution—like the advent of the "silent spring"—has occurred as a result of the computer and related electronic advances which are shaking the pillars of Western civilization's value structures, economic systems, and political orders. Although it has been given a number of descriptive names—the Post-Industrial Order, the Service Society, and the Knowledge Explosion—the current upheaval is fanned mainly by two major developments: advances in molecular biology and the spread of computer technology. That the first slipped softly into the mainstreams of our consciousness is illustrated by the Gordon Conference which was convened to dis-

*Charles Lamont Post Distinguished Professor, The American College; Adjunct Professor of Business, Columbia University

cuss the significance of research in nucleic acids and in recombinant DNA. Except for reporters and a few lawyers, there was, outside the scientists themselves, little popular interest. Reasons for this lack of concern are easy to find: there were no genuine historical precedents for this new revolution; the research appeared extremely esoteric; the people had come to accept spectacular scientific advances as routine.

However, the power of molecular biology was unlike the power of other advances in science and the experts knew that a storm was coming. What was needed to arouse the public to the socioethical issues involved in DNA experiments was leadership. And when this came from the scientific community itself, the public responded quickly. Scientists who objected to further intensive DNA research went before lay groups to point out some possible consequence of this research: that recombinant DNA for microorganisms might be absorbed in human cells in such a way as to engender malignant changes; that pathogenic bacteria might be induced to expand beyond their present domains; that benign bacteria, present in human beings, might produce new chemicals toxic to mankind; and that pathogens thus inadvertently created might escape into an environment where their spread would be irreversible. At this time the basic shape of the debate over molecular biology's implications is just beginning to form but, even in these early steps, policymakers know that historic decisions will be made.

THE COMPUTER

The second revolution is spelled out in what is now a household word—the computer. While it promises no pyrotechnical burst of the magnitude offered by molecular biology, it also will influence the lives of countless individuals—their values, the private organizations they create, and the way they govern themselves. While we are no longer blind to the computer's permeative influence, few have clear visions of the computer's ultimate consequences.

The computer is shorthand for an array of electronic applications—word processing, microprocessing in manufacturing and engineering, and the like. The French have coined one word to cover this expanding waterfront: *telematics*. Since it has the virtue of incorporating, more adequately than does our word computer, the multidimensional nature of the electronic revolutions, the term "telematics" will be used in this essay. No great difference in meaning, however, exists between telematics and postindustrialism, the term made popular by Daniel Bell, because Bell defined the postindustrial society as one "in which telecommunications and computers are strategic for the exchange of information and knowledge"; the difference, as a consequence, between the industrial order and the postindustrial order is that the former is based on machine technology and the latter on intellectual technology.[1]

How rapidly the telematics revolution is moving may be illustrated by a brief review of history. It was only fifteen short years ago, in 1956, that a simple statistic revealed a turning point in history: for the first time in the life of any industrial civilization, white-collar workers outnumbered blue-collar employees. The movement started at the end of World War II when the number of workers in industry began to decline; as these workers were replaced by automation, the number of technicians increased and jobs were upgraded. One company's experience is a mirror of many others. When Western Electric moved away from electromechanical equipment to electronic switching gear for the phone company, a startling change in the work force force occurred. Before the change at its Northern Illinois facility, blue-collar workers outnumbered white-collar workers three to one. Today the ratio is one to one.[2] In this fast-growing group, the fastest growing sector consists of technical and professional employees—well-educated people who are giving a new dimension to the American work force.

Organizations, no less than individuals, are driven into new forms and structures by telematics. Production is often defined as a process where people huddle around a computer, but if the computer is located in a worker's home—the "electronic cottage"—there is no longer any need to huddle. The organization of work is thereby profoundly altered. Examples tell the story.

In the financial services field, American Express is moving to acquire the investment company Shearson Loeb Rhoades in order to enhance its role in finance as an electronics supermarket. Prudential Insurance has already acquired another investment firm, Bache and Company. Both of the corporate movements—one planned and the other completed—illustrate dramatically an important fact, namely, that technology is making the law obsolescent. On the darker side, the new technology makes possible more effective terrorist assaults on corporate and government leadership because access to nuclear materials or sabotage of vital computers holds the potential for bringing down the social order.[3]

Does History Help?

Fearful of the havoc that might be induced by the telematics and molecular biology revolutions, leaders naturally seek solace from history. But the effort is not overly promising as a cursory review of the major revolutions indicate. The commercial revolution of the sixteenth century, the religious revolution of the seventeenth century, and the industrial revolution of the eighteenth century were all accompanied by violence. In the first, city states like Genoa and Venice, and nation states like England and Holland, fought bloody wars for commercial ascendency. The religious revolution triggered the Thirty Years War, which ended in 1648 with the Treaty of Westphalia; peace, however, was made possible only because Protestants and Catholics were too exhausted to continue the bloddy struggle and too stubborn to accept genuine compromise. Finally, the industrial revolution of late nineteenth-century America was marked by over fifty years of "civil wars" when rag-tag troops (described variously as the Molly McGuires and the Pinkertons, the Coal and Iron Police and the steelmen) clashed in bloody encounters in Pennsylvania's mining and steel towns.

Past revolutions raise an important question for contemporary society: can it avoid the divisiveness, the tumult, the bloodshed that accompanied previous revolutions? If so, how? Prophecies regarding the impact of telematics on individuals and on society offer the extremes of apocalypse and of utopia. As so often happens when experts gather to discuss a complicated issue, nonexperts are treated to a variety of different views. Hope and fear, optimism and pessimism, confidence and despair, are liberally interspersed in the various analyses.

THE PROPHECIES

In this analysis initial emphasis will be more on the grim possibilities, not because pessimists have better arguments but because they raise danger signals which force us into a more intensive search for constructive solutions. I propose to address the debate by stating some disturbing conclusions advanced here by computer-wise people which I will follow with a brief set of counterarguments.

Six "gloomy" propositions emerged at the Bentley Conference.

1. *Telematics will increase unemployment and, by so doing, add an unbearable burden to a society already wracked by "slump-fation."*

2. *Computer technology's enormous potential is not being used to meet human needs, and corporate America must be held guilty for deliberately withholding supply until the market is ready to*

*provide handsome profits. The corporate profile of the future is
the "Chrysler-Hooker" syndrome.*

3. *The computer revolution will diminish individual freedom
   because—*
   a. *information and knowledge, the most significant forms of con-
      temporary property, are passing from individuals to organiza-
      tions; and*
   b. *computers are invading individual privacy so that a person's
      home is not a castle but a prison.*

4. *Knowledge is power, yet more and more Americans are becoming powerless because—*
   a. *the determination of what constitutes information essential to
      policymaking will be made by small cadres of "information re-
      source managers" (IRM) who monitor the information streams,
      and*
   b. *people who control critical data control the organization.*

5. *Organizations, driven by competition and by more advanced
   computerization, are establishing precise codes of ethics which
   will supersede the ethics of individuals within the organization.
   The supporting argument is simple:*
   a. *When an individual joins an enterprise, such a person accepts
      the roles, rules, and goals of the organization; and*
   b. *If there is a clash between organizational and individual ethics,
      the former will prevail.*

6. *The Judeo-Christian moral tradition has failed contemporary
   man. Joseph Coates put it bluntly when he said that religion is
   a bust.*[4] *If the Nietzschean argument (God is dead) is not widely
   accepted, the Kierkegaardian thesis (Christianity is dead) is.*

It now becomes appropriate to comment briefly on each generali-
zation.

Job Opportunities

The Thesis. When we are told that the office of the future will
consist of few machines and one human, that computers will provide in seconds what x-ray technicians perform in hours, that trains
will be run from New York to Chicago without benefit of even a
single engineer, the inference is clear: a computer-intensive society
will throw millions out of work. The supporting argument runs
along these lines: while America's business system can generate
some 63.4 million full-time jobs, over 27 percent are held by persons

(mainly women) earning less than $10,000 per year. This is the army of unskilled workers whose vulnerability to layoffs is intensified by telematics. In 1979 a disproportionate amount of the $1.3 trillion available for wages and salaries went to the information workers; furthermore, many technologically intensive industries do not create employment opportunities for dispossessed workers. California's "Silicon Valley" (a center of the semiconductor industry) is offered as the perfect example; few dispossessed Youngstown Steel or General Motors workers will find employment in the Silicon Valleys of the world.

Antithesis. While the prospect of massive job dislocations is real, the probability of massive unemployment occasioned by the computer is less likely. It is instructive to recall the dire predictions made a decade or two ago to the effect that mid-management ranks would be leveled by computers, which would think faster, decide better, and communicate more effectively than their human counterparts. The results have simply not worked out as predicted. As a matter of fact, Professor Brian Quinn of Dartmouth has argued (Chapter 7A) that the demand for technology has increased in the order of two thousand since its inception and that America's future export patterns will be overwhelmingly in computers—and, one might add, in foodstuffs. Foreign competitors may continue to produce automobiles and steel more efficiently, but there is no evidence of their superiority in the production of computers. As a result, the job market should actually improve. There is further cause for optimism. While the secretary's job and the scientist's job are made simpler, the manufacture of such machines has become infinitely more complex. With even the most remote appreciation of the present job market, one recognizes the scarcities of electrical engineering and computer maintenance people.

Computers will not add to unemployment. They may, on the other hand, fail to relieve it, and optimism over job prospects in America's future must be guarded. People denied work become frustrated and angry. In the 1960s American blacks took to the streets to vent their frustration over denial to political rights; in the 1980s whites and blacks may take to the streets to demand economic rights. These groups will comprise not the army of unemployed displaced by computers but, rather, existing cadres that cannot secure jobs because they are functionally illiterate. Such groups will also consist of those who will be displaced by the uneven pace and sequencing of computer technology into the mainstream of American production, and this problem will be aggravated if displaced workers are not given opportunities—well before the introduction of new technology—for new training. If the nation's old assignment continues, namely, job creation, the new assignment is for better job preparation.

Corporate Villainy

The Thesis. There is little need to rehash the fact that American businessmen, especially those associated with large enterprises, are losing favor with the American people. The United States Chamber of Commerce noted in its Spring 1981 catalog that public confidence in business is just one point above the all-time low of 1974 in the Harris Polls. Since this is the case, the relevant questions are these: Is the public confused because it is misled? Or is the public correct because business fails? By and large, scholars tend to agree with the public on the basis of evidence that includes corporate bribery, pollution, declining productivity rates, irresponsible plant closures, defective products, and the like. Ralph Nader is the best known critic of corporate behavior and "Naderism" has become a household word.[5] If Nader pleads to give the free market a chance to work, Joseph Coates concludes that it will not work—and probably cannot work—in the computer field. The unsatisfied needs of the nation's handicapped (which he estimated to be approximately a third of the population) reveals to him the sorry fact that hunger for the almighty dollar has dulled appreciation of the needs of the less fortunate. Coates underscores his point by citing a typical corporate response when the pollution issue is raised: deny culpability. The Hooker Corporation made "Love Canal" a hated term. Pollution of water is followed by pollution of truth.

The reason why such irresponsibilities will continue, according to Coates (and why the public can expect little relief from enlightened leadership in the private sector) is due to "turnover at the top." In corporate America the top executive lasts no more than six years (more likely four), and he lives in a world surrounded by eight other eager beavers whose hands are outstretched for the brass ring of power. Thirty years' experience with a single corporation, dominated by a philosophy of no boat rocking, paralyzes courage and warps moral vision. This, in brief, is the belief of the "Coatesians" among us.

Antithesis. Because the indictment is so damning and so widely believed, it is important to introduce another perspective lest the very parochialism attributed to corporate executives becomes the hallmark of the critics themselves. Is the market inefficient? If it is, why do automobile managers and workers unite in a belief that

Toyota is a dirty word? If the free market in telematics is imprisoned by greedy oligarchs, how can we explain medical instrumentation which brings more efficient diagnosis and care? The first-quarter IBM report for 1981 carried news of two high-performance analytical instruments. One is a microprocessor-controlled liquid chromatograph, the LC/9533, developed to help chemists separate complex mixtures into component parts. It has many applications in research and development, in quality control and environmental analysis. Another is the IR/85, which offers many previously available features at considerably lower cost. Designed to analyze gases, liquids, and solids, the IR/85 has a broad range of applications in the pharmaceutical, food, petrochemical, semiconductor, and biomedical fields. Parenthetically, IBM reported that it employs several thousand handicapped and that special plans are being developed to extend employment opportunities during the 1981 United Nation International Year of Disabled Persons.

Corporate pollution is the other charge and the assault on environment is not a happy page in our history. Indifference bordering on contempt for physical nature has been part and parcel of American development. The farmers of the American West, unlike the peasants of Europe, ravaged their lands ruthlessly. Mythologizing of frontier heroes like Davey Crockett did not blind historian Vernon Parrington to his less appealing side and what it represented:

> Wastefulness was in his frontier blood and Davey was a true frontier wastrel.... With his pack of hounds he slaughtered with amazing efficiency. His hundred and five bears in a single season, his six deer shot in one day while pursuing other game (two of which were left hanging in the woods) serve to explain why the rich hunting grounds of the Indians were swept so quickly bare of game by the white invaders. Davey was but one of thousands who were wasting the resources of the Inland Empire.[6]

Business buccaneers continued the wasteful traditions. The conclusion is clear: in the past nearly all Americans have been found to treat nature unkindly. To cite history, however, is not to excuse. Refineries and chemical plants can do more damage in one minute than Davey Crockett could do all year. So today's problem is more acute and the worries more justified. To use the Hooker Corporation, however, as typical of the entire American industry is to turn characterization into caricature. If management at Hooker is bad, can the same thing be said of IBM and Texas Instruments, of General Electric and Xerox, of Hewlett Packard and Genentech? It is dangerous to conclude that the sickness among the few means a cancer in all.

Personal Liberty

Fears have been expressed that telematics will erode individual freedom since information systems are becoming the property of large organizations and because personal privacy is so easily invaded by owners of computer-based record systems. A comment on each follows.

Property-Freedom. The relationship of freedom to private property has been asserted by medievalists, by John Locke, and by our constitutional framers. When Locke was writing—and when, later, American politicians were forming the Constitution—the economy rested upon an extractive base; it was therefore easy to accept the conclusion that anyone who mixed his or her individuality with nature's gift to produce a socially useful product had a right to the resultant product. Private property was essential to survival and the capacity to excel in its enlargement was viewed as a mark of superior quality. The property class, so it was asserted, was rightfully the ruling class.

Today, however, knowledge is property and if knowledge belongs to computer owners, will not the fundamental bulwarks of freedom collapse? Answers are unclear. Courts have been requested to determine when an idea belongs to an individual and when it belongs to an organization. Generally speaking, the results have been to favor knowledge as corporate property when it has been generated by team research with funds provided by the enterprise. The reasoning seems to be, at least superficially, persuasive. Just as nonskilled workers sell their muscle to a firm in return for wages so, too, do knowledge workers sell their ideas to the enterprise. A *quid pro quo* is at work.

There is restiveness over the judiciary's approach. A revealing question was raised by Jeffrey Meldman of MIT who asked: "Is not knowledge a fundamental part of the human personality in a way that muscle is not?" A person may lose a finger or a leg—and the loss hurts; but if a person loses ideas generated by the mind, the loss is irreparable. The reason is that a "muscle-demanding world" is substantially different from a "thought-demanding world." Meldman's question has relevance to the observations of George Cabot Lodge: "While a person may get certain psychic kicks out of owning a jewel or a car or a television set or a house, does it really make a substantive difference to own or rent? There is a new right which clearly supersedes in political and social importance. It is the right to survive—to enjoy property rights, income, health, and other rights associated with membership in the American community."[7]

So far as the computer is involved, should the right to enjoy the knowledge so developed belong to the owner of the idea? Or to the owner of the computer which extends the "idea man's capacity to think"? When it is manifestly impossible to identify precisely each individual's contribution to the product of team research, when it is difficult to measure how far humans can go without benefit of computers, when it is difficult to assign full value to a research facility, it is hard to know how to isolate, recognize, and reward the various claimants. On balance, it appears as though the courts are moving in the right direction because they examine problems in the light of specific circumstances. Public and corporate planning, however, must take these step-by-step judicial decisions and forge them into an overall policy that gives guidance to individuals and to organizations on "what is mine" and "what is theirs."

Privacy. If the property relationship between individual and corporate knowledge is difficult to determine, the privacy issue may be even more complex. Not that telematics has created the privacy policy. In our constitutional history we had rulings initially on defamation and, later, on protection of the press. In an old 1796 case the court held that everyone has "a right to keep his sentiments private if he so pleases." The classic statement on privacy was made in 1890 by Samuel D. Warren and Louis D. Brandeis.[8] The two men were law partners at a time when the Warren family became subject to detailed gossipy newspaper accounts of family social affairs. Angered by the emotional harm visited upon the family, Warren and Brandeis wrote an article whose opening salvo is worth quoting in detail:

> That the individual shall have full protection in person and in property is a principle as old as the common law; but it has been found necessary from time to time to define anew the exact nature and extent of such protection. Political, social, and economic changes entail the recognition of new rights, and the common law, in its eternal youth, grows to meet the demands of society.
>
> Clearly the question of whether our law will recognize and protect the right to privacy.... must soon come before our courts for consideration.

Of the desirability—indeed of the necessity—of some such protection, there can, it is believed, be no doubt. The press is overstepping in every direction the obvious bounds of propriety and of decency. Gossip is no longer the resource of the idle and of the vicious, but has become a trade, which is pursued with industry as well as effrontery. To satisfy a prurient taste, the details of sexual relations are spread broadcast in the columns of the daily papers. To occupy the indolent, column upon column is filled with idle gossip, which can only be procured by intrusion upon the domestic circle ... When personal gossip attains the dignity of print, and crowds the space available for matters of real interest to the community, what wonder that the ignorant and thoughtless mistake its relative importance. Easy of comprehension, appealing to that weak side of human nature which is never wholly cast down by the misfortunes and frailties of our neighbors, no one can be surprised that it usurps the place of interest in brains capable of other things. Triviality destroys at once robustness of thought and delicacy of feeling. No enthusiasm can flourish, no generous impulse can survive under its blighting influence.[9]

The lawyers asserted the need of common law to adjust to new circumstances; telematics is also forcing barristers and judges to seek new accommodations in the law. Prospects for privacy's triumph are not assured because the early defense of privacy rights over the public's right to know has been sharply modified. In 1964 the Supreme Court declared that journalistic carelessness was a defense even when it published lies about a public official.[10] Four years later, the Court declared that to assure publication of truth on public issues, it is essential for the First Amendment to protect some erroneous as well as true statements.[11] Americans in 1980 are really left in an awkward position because the privacy issue has been only partially resolved. Where, then, do we stand now?

The attempt to assassinate President Reagan dramatizes the contemporary issue. Within a few hours after the assault two hundred million Americans knew more about the assailant's recent past than did his parents. That is because computers establish effective audit trails on individuals—their behavior patterns, their social and professional affiliations, their acquaintances, and the like. Computers store arrest records which, for efficiency's sake, are brief—and therefore inadequate and often misleading as Arthur Miller has pointed out.[12]

Because of their need to acquire information on people, insurance companies are especially suspect. Recently one insurance company hired a polling organization to test the depth of American feeling on the issue of privacy. Eighty percent of those surveyed felt that computerized personal information was not adequately safeguarded; 88 percent criticized credit institutions for their inadequacies and for improper sharing of the information they collect; 76 percent believed that Americans surrendered their privacy the day they opened their first charge accounts. By an eight-to-one majority, these Americans expressed the belief that institutionalization of credit and the computerization of information had made it much easier to obtain and transmit information improperly about the individuals and their personal lives.

The scale of computer operation is mammoth. American Express has over ten million credit cards in effect throughout the world and these credit cards provided $902,000,000 of revenue during the first nine months of 1979. Using American Express as an example, critical questions arise. Should the company release demographic information which shows spending patterns if other businesses are willing to pay for it? Should it invest in more costly computer systems to assure privacy protection by controlling accessibility to data and mailing lists? It is estimated that the average American has dealings linked to a computer at least ten times a day. Since the computer memory storage is advanced to a point where one memory can store 470 billion characters of data (the equivalent of 2,000 sets of twenty-three-volume *Encyclopedia Brittanica*), it is obvious that when more data are stored about individuals, more information can be released on individuals.

The Linowes Commission on Privacy opened its analysis of the insurance relationship with these words, "The activities of the nation's 4,700 insurance companies touch the lives of all Americans in a variety of ways."[13] Nearly 90 percent of the civilian population under age 65 is covered by individual or group policies. Insurers must evaluate people, their property, and their economic potential; they must seek information about individuals and, in the process, become the largest gatherers and users of data. To secure information, the companies often rely on the Medical Information Bureau (MIB), a nonincorporated, nonprofit trade association set up to expedite the transfer of medical record information among life insurers. The MIB managers insist that the receiving insurance company never base an adverse underwriting decision on information received from MIB but that it must take its own independent assessment. Since, however, vast amounts of information about individuals flow through the MIB system, there is always fear in some quarters over leakage.

The data flow is no longer a small river. In addition, there is a fire marshall reporting service, an automobile theft bureau reporting system, a crime prevention institute, and a host of like agencies.[14] None of the private record-gathering groups compares in scope to the activities of governmental bureaus, especially the Federal Bureau of Investigation, the Secret Service, and the Census Bureau. Sensitive to their powers, the Commerce Department has established an Office of Federal Statistic Policy Standards and the Federal Paperwork Commission. In a 1978 report one reassuring observation was made on the privacy issue:

> Computers, however, also provide new capacities for protecting individual data. Once the data are in a machine-readable medium, individual and geographic identifiers can be removed from the records. The data can then be made available to interested parties with the confidentiality of the data safeguarded. Data can be encrypted much more easily in a computer system than by hand. This provides more protection to personal privacy and data confidentiality than the manual systems of yesteryear.[15]

That the privacy issue is far from a satisfactory resolution is illustrated by the California "live-birth" incident. In 1978 the State decided to seek more information about maternal drug and alcohol use and its relationship to the condition of the new born infant. After a series of compromises, a bill was approved by the California Legislature in 1978. What the legislature had to do was walk through a maze of conflicting claims made on behalf of individuals and on behalf of the State. For individuals the birth certificate had a certain benefit as an important legal document used to prove facts about age, parentage, and citizenship: it is useful for school entrance, voter registration, passport applications, welfare eligibility, and many other things. But the State also has its interests since policy requires careful planning, evaluation, and research.

California also had an "open records" law which allowed persons to inspect the data. In order to preclude too much interference from the "open-records" approach, California passed regulations to control access. The result was unintended—and disturbing. Parents were prevented from learning much about their own offspring while researchers had almost unlimited access. Caught in the cross-current, a new rule was passed which exempted birth certificates from the open-records law and required a researcher wishing to use the data to go through an intensive review process. To assure confidentiality, fines and jail sentences were provided and those responsible for disclosures are subject to civil and criminal damages if harm occurs. The result? Critics argue, on one side, that the California system opens too much private information to public scrutiny. Critics from another perspective insist that the State can no longer provide accurate information on such important items as infant mortality, reproductive rates by race, the impact of urban environment on health, and similar matters.[16]

In a sense the California story is the country's story. The long reach of computer "fingers" simply intensifies the problem. As courts and legislatures react on an *ad hoc* basis, expectations are that public officials will develop a reasonable, if not ideal, balance between the individual's right to privacy and the public's right to know. As the process unfolds there is bound to be legitimate fear that if carelessness exculpates the media from legal responsibility, might not carelessness be used by the Supreme Court as a defense against charges of other unwarranted invasions of privacy? Certainly it is no harsh judgment on the Supreme Court to say, simply, that it was wrong in the *New York Times* decision of 1964.[17] One may expect, therefore, considerable debate and further litigation on the privacy issue. Meanwhile the computer sits as culprit for forms of negligence to which it has made only partial contributions. It sits vulnerable because few consistent precedents are available to guide policymakers on the privacy issue.

An arresting new developing meriting special attention is the growth of the Information Resource Management (IRM) movement. Experienced people like Elizabeth Byrne Adams and W. Forest Horton are acutely aware that complex decision making is rendered less effective by the Niagara of data swamping today's organizations. On the other hand, critics of the IRM group see them as a super elite among the knowledge elite. If the latter has great power, must not the former have even more? Having more, are they not more dangerous?

In this highly charged debate two questions must be addressed. The first asks whether or not Information Resource Management is essential to the effectiveness of large organizations; the second asks whether such great powers over information gathering and information using can be controlled in the public interests? To the first question the answer is yes. Organizations leaders, whether in the private or the public sector, simply cannot handle the mass of detail that flows through the information stream in their respective organizations. Someone is needed to sort out—and the sorting out process requires a sophisticated understanding of the organization's structure and purpose. The second question is more complex.

Relatively small numbers of highly trained experts in a staff position control the data flow. Will its staff behavior pattern become like other staff behavior patterns where staff needs are often placed ahead of organizational needs? Will the IRM groups be willing to open their operations to public scrutiny? Will such review invite meddling by the uninformed, sensationalism by "investigative" journalists, and intervention by public authorities? The worries are not to be dismissed lightly.

Perhaps it is well to revert to the basic principle laid down by Warren and Brandeis in 1890. While their conclusion, on first blush, seems little more than an expression of common sense and fair play, it can provide the starting point for further analysis: *a person's inner life is sacred.* After all, the 1890 essay was little more than a reassertion of this first principle and its application to secondary effects.

Organizational/Individual Code of Ethics

Because of definitional ambiguities regarding fiduciary responsibilities both in ethics and in law, it is predictable that organizations will seek to establish more precise codes of conduct to guide their agents when problems of property rights and privacy claims arise. While there is no universal enthusiasm for the formulation of such codes, there is little practical opposition to their enactment. When, however, assumptions are made to the effect that institutional codes are intrinsically and necessarily superior to an individual's ethic, problems arise. Behind the assumption of organizational "superiority" is a logic which holds that when an individual voluntarily joins an organization that individual accepts the role, the rule, and the goals of the enterprise.

John Ladd is one expert who argues that large organizations "are governed by social standards of conduct that sever to guide, justify and explain a particular action of corporate officisls. [Such] standards must by their very nature deviate in significant ways from moral standards that govern the conduct of individual persons. As a consequence, many people in our society find themselves under a double standard of morality: one at work and the other at home with friends and neighbors. The resulting tension produces what could be called a 'moral schizophrenia'."[18]

Ladd's argument tilts toward granting priority to the organization ethic because every organization must be seen as a single-entity decision maker. The implication, of course, is that since enterprises have their own rules, individuals may be insulated from the more significant moral impacts of their own actions. A thesis against the Ladd argument has been posed and ably developed by Kenneth Goodpaster, who insisted that individuals, as moral persons, can never be excused from responsibility; such responsibility extends not simply to interpersonal relationships but to organizational and interorganizational relationships as well.[19]

Of immediate relevance is not the definitive resolution of the debate but recognition of the fact that important and thoughtful people subscribe to the theory that the organizational ethic is independent of individual morality and that, as a consequence, when conflict erupts between the firm and the individual, the conflict must be resolved in favor of the enterprise. Some critics say that such logic drives people to a "fink-and-funk" morality. The "finks" are the whistle blowers who are alternately hailed and damned by society; the "funks" are those who "cop out" by shirking organizational duties that such individuals find ethically repugnant. Scholarship is challenged to update and refine the concepts of fiduciary responsibility so that the individual-societal relationship comes into clear light. A happy omen may be found in the growing number of scholars who are addressing this ethical problem and the growing number of organizations that recognize the need to provide mechanisms (due process, open door) that can ajudicate peacefully differences between the individual and the organization.

Judeo-Christian Traditions

Deeply upsetting to "traditionalists" is the number of people voicing their skepticism of traditional religious values. Not infrequently the skepticism borders on contempt. According to the critics, religious traditions have outlived their usefulness; churches have failed; worship is a liturgical charade; religious morality is a bust. These emanations are encouraged by a society evolving from a mythological toward a technological civilization. The consequence of that transformation is momentous to any understanding of human nature itself. The old soteriological approach (which stressed the importance of a divinity for eternal salvation) is replaced by an eschatological understanding of human nature which holds that the ultimate destiny of mankind is to move through an evolutionary process to some yet-to-be-understood goal.

Compounding a problem already serious is the nature of the new technology. In times past, technology was a tool that expanded man's capacities; today technology is a complex method for doing things man alone cannot do. As a result, the instrument may alter the man. Contemporary individuals seem to have lost interest in their souls and regained interest in how cybernetics and other electronic programs can change man himself. Herbert Simon, Nobel Laureate in economics, recently expressed the view that greater understanding of the computer's potential and progress in artificial intelligence mean that humans must recognize that the brain is a complicated machine not too dissimilar from the computer. In a companion piece Daniel Bell suggested that because knowledge will have to be in a syntax acceptable to computers if it is to rate as knowledge, knowledge must have a mathematical dimension.[20] If thinking is a unique characteristic of persons and if computers can think, are computers persons? Or are persons machines? Are humans required to refashion not only a new meaning for knowledge but a new meaning of themselves? Max Horkheimer made a telling statement in his important book, *Eclipse of Reason,* when he wrote:

> Justice, equality, happiness, tolerance—all the concepts that . . . were in preceding centuries supposed to be inherent in or sanctioned by reason, have lost their intellectual roots . . . . Endorsed by venerable historical documents, they may still enjoy a certain prestige, and some are contained in the supreme law of the greatest countries. Nevertheless, they lack any confirmation by reason in its modern sense. Who can say that any of these ideals is more closely related to truth than its opposite? *According to the philosophy of the average modern intellectual, there is only one authority, namely, science, conceived as the classification of facts and the calculation of probabilities.* The statement that justice and freedom are better in themselves than injustice and oppression is scientifically unverifiable and useless.[21]

The impact of the new technology on past religious traditions is explained in a variety of ways, but the essential elements of the new religiosity are revealed in the following propositions:

1. Since God is conceived by man, all concepts of God reflect cultural presuppositions.
2. When the culture collapses (as it is now collapsing as life moves from the mythological to the technological), the traditional God becomes a thing of the past which, like all superfluities, must die.
3. The death of God not only signifies an estrangement from old traditions but reflects a cultural crisis bearing on man's understanding of himself.

4. Whereas the Judeo-Christian tradition asserted that God is the cause of all existence and that the universe exhibits purposiveness, the new culture asserts that God not only cannot be taken for granted but that the world is not necessarily meaningful. Meaning is a datum, not a mandate.

The ultimate conclusion from the foregoing is powerful: ethical values, once conceived as reinforcing man's given nature, cannot be assumed to be normative until they are refashioned in ways that permit men to surpass themselves and to go beyond what an alleged God-given nature has determined.[22] Perhaps an understanding of the difference between the "new" philosophy and the "old" theology can be gleaned from the way the Supreme Court has handled affirmative action. In a series of cases, the Court held that discrimination on the basis of race is wrong because it denies black citizens access to material goods and services. Injury becomes the criterion. If this is so, then one must ask whether the law requires evidence of material injuries before it is justified in acting? Religious tradition would answer clearly in the negative—and for these reasons:

Man is a moral being whose relationship with others is not determined solely by taste or individual preference.

Since an individual's birth and death are not under that individual's total control, there must be another power superior to man.

Because man is an economic being, the world of scarcity is a datum of existence, not an artifact.

The traditional argument's ultimate logic is found in the Declaration of Independence, which acknowledges a Divine Creator and recognizes man as a moral and contingent being. The traditional religious ethic makes several points that are not accepted today in certain parts of the world. Among the maxims from the Judeo-Christian tradition are these: humans may not be—wantonly and indiscriminately—slaughtered; persons cannot be arbitrarily imprisoned; individuals may not be ruthlessly exploited; parents cannot casually discard children—or be casually discarded by children; orphans may not be robbed of their birthright; a person's reputation may not be falsely impugned; and privacy may not be invaded indiscriminately by outsiders. Even a cursory examination of the foregoing indicates that the old traditions spoke to issues that still confront us, albeit in new guises, such as liberty, privacy, property, personhood. To assert that the Judeo-Christian tradition has no relevance to contemporary problems because of the computer is to go beyond the bounds of history and of logic.

The differences between the old and new approaches to morality may be gleaned from two positions articulated by two brilliant observers of our times. The first is Victor Weisskopf, Institute Professor of Physics at MIT. Remarking on the decay of previously existing sources of meaning and purpose, Weisskopf spoke of a "big void in our bellies, a void that craves to be filled." However, the grandest creations and achievements of modern science serve as inspirational sources only to a small minority of humans; their values seem to be not suitable for a wider spread. The larger majority cannot get meaning, sense, and purpose from these sources. They must have some sort of religion. Goethe's observation is recalled:

> He who has Art and Science
> Has also a religion
> But those who do not have them
> Better have religion[23]

The beauty of the foregoing observation cannot obscure the unstated premise, namely, that religion is for lesser intellects. The sought-after God is scientific truth and empiricism is the hunter. Horkheimer's modern man is at work, speaking softly—even poetically—in the contemporary idiom.

The older view finds concordance in a different insight. C. S. Lewis, in one essay, described man as consisting not simply of head, but of head, chest, and belly. The chest is the source of magnanimity and of sentiment and is the indispensable liaison between cerebral man and visual man.

> It may even be said that it is by this middle element that man is man: for by his intellect he is mere spirit and by his appetite mere animal. The operation of *The Green Book* [presumably the secularist's text] and its kind is to produce what may be called Men without Chests .... It is an outrage that they should be commonly spoken of as Intellectuals. This gives them the chance to say that he who attacks them attacks Intelligence. It is not so. They are not distinguished from other men by any unusual skill in finding truth nor any virginal ardour to pursue her. Indeed it would be strange if they were: a persevering devotion to truth, a nice sense of intellectual honour, cannot be long maintained without the aid of a sentiment .... and the sentiment makes room for magnanimity and magnanimity is the special gift of Divinity to man.[24]

Disorder, bordering on anarchy, exists in the contemporary world of values. Is that condition due to a failure of religion? Or a failure of secularism? What Weiskopf and Lewis have done is to cast an old debate into an exciting, new, and unexpected world.

CONCLUSIONS

In our contemporary world some long-standing issues have been positioned in more dramatic forms than ever. The computer throws new light on old problems and new shadows on old lights. Telematics is of inestimable value because it forces all of us to re-think some fundamental questions: What is a human person? What are fundamental human rights? What is a moral community? Where is the postindustrial world leading us?

Civilization is in the making. We are its makers. In that new creation some of our mentors call us to abandon the old religious tradition—because it is a bust—and embrace the new. Others in the traditional mold urge us to cling stubbornly—like the "plain folk of Pennsylvania"—to the old. Perhaps the prudent course is to attend carefully to the advice of Professor of Computer Science Joseph Weizenbaum of MIT:

> I want my students (and everyone) to have heard me affirm that the computer is a powerful new metaphor for helping us to understand many aspects of the world, but that it enslaves the mind that has no other metaphors and few other resources to call on. The world is many things, and no single framework is large enough to contain them all, neither that of man's science nor that of his poetry, neither that of man's science nor that of his poetry, neither that of calculating reason nor that of pure intuition. And just as a love of music does not suffice to enable one to play the violin—one must also master the craft of the instrument and of music itself—so it is not enough to love humanity in order to help it survive. The teacher's calling to teach his craft is therefore an honorable one. But he must do more than that: he must teach more than one metaphor, and he must teach more by the example of his conduct than by what he writes on the blackboard. He must teach the limitations of his tools as well as their power.[25]

In the long race between man and computer, the former appears to be crawling and the computer sprinting. Is man the tortoise and the computer the hare? One hopes so. Does one know so?

If the question is unanswered, we may wind up calculating everything—and valuing nothing.

NOTES

1. Daniel Bell, *The Coming of the Post-Industrial Society* (New York: Basic Books, Inc., 1976) pp. xii–xiii.
2. Alvin Toffler, *The Third Wave* (New York: Bantam Books, 1980). See Chapter 16.
3. On this point see Ernest Evans, *Calling a Truce to Terror* (Westport, Conn.: Greenwood Press, 1980), and R. C. Clark, *Technological Terrorism* (Old Greenwich, Conn.: Devin-Adair, 1979).
4. Chapter 1, p. 3.
5. Ralph Nader et al., "Who Rules the Great Corporations?" *Business and Society Review* (Summer 1976), pp. 40–49.
6. Vernon Louis Parrington, *Main Currents in American Thought* (New York: Harcourt Brace and Co., 1930), Vol. 2, p. 179.
7. George Cabot Lodge, "Managerial Implications of Ideological Change," in Clarence C. Walton, ed., *The Ethics of Corporate Conduct* (Englewood Cliffs, N.J.: Prentice-Hall, 1977), p. 91.
8. Samuel D. Warren and Louis D. Brandeis, "The Right to Privacy," *Harvard Law Review,* Vol. 4 (1890), pp. 193–220.
9. Ibid., pp. 193, 196.
10. New York Times Company *v.* Sullivan (376 U.S. 254).
11. St. Amant *v.* Thompson (390 U.S. 727).
12. Arthur Miller, *The Assault on Privacy* (New York: The New York American Library, 1972). See also the important studies by Alan Westin, *Privacy and Freedom* (London: Bodley Head, 1970) and James Rule et al., *The Politics of Privacy: Planning for Personal Data Systems as Powerful Technologies* (New York: Elsevier, 1980).
13. *The Report of the Privacy Protection Study Commission* (Washington, D.C.: GPO, 1977), p. 159. Relevant is Alan Westin's study, *Data Banks in a Free Society* (New York: Times Publishing Co., 1972).
14. See *The Life Insurance Fact Book* (New York: The American Council of Life Insurance, 1976) and *Insurance Facts* (New York: The Insurance Information Institute, 1976).
15. U.S. Department of Commerce Office of Federal Statistical Policy and Standards, *Statistical Policy Working Paper 2* (Appendix B), p. 61.
16. C. Hexter and W. Winkelstein, "California's New Birth Certificate Law: A Model for the Nation?" *The American Journal of Public Health,* Vol. 69 (1979), pp. 704–715.
17. New York Times Company *v.* Sullivan (376 U.S. 254).
18. Quoted from W. Michael Hoffman, ed., *Proceedings of the Second National Conference on Business Ethics* (Waltham, Mass.: Bentley College, 1978), pp. 103–104.
19. Ibid., pp. 99–101.
20. See Simon's and Bell's essays in Tom Forester, ed., *The Microelectronic Revolution* (Cambridge, Mass.: The M.I.T. Press, 1980).
21. Max Horkheimer, *Eclipse of Reason* (New York: Seabury Press, 1974), pp. 23–24. Italics added.
22. Gabriel Vahanian, "Technological Utopianism in the Future of Religion," *Syracuse Scholar,* Vol. 1 (1980), pp. 44–48.
23. Victor Weisskopf, "Art and Science," *The American Scholar,* Vol. 48 (Autumn 1979), p. 483.
24. C. S. Lewis, *The Abolition of Man* (New York: The Macmillan Co., 1957), p. 16.
25. Joseph Weizenbaum, *Computer Power and Human Reason* (San Francisco: W. H. Freeman Co., 1976), p. 277.

About the Editors

W. Michael Hoffman is Director of the Center for Business Ethics and Chair of the Philosophy Department at Bentley College. He received his Ph.D. in philosophy from the University of Massachusetts at Amherst. Hoffman has published numerous articles in various professional journals and has lectured on metaphysics, philosophy of religion, business ethics, philosophical ecology, and the history of ideas. In addition, he is the author of *Kant's Theory of Freedom: A Metaphysical Inquiry.* Hoffman has received grants from the National Endowment for the Humanities, the Matchette Foundation, and the Council for Philosophical Studies.

Jennifer Mills Moore is Research Associate at the Center for Business Ethics and Adjunct Instructor of Philosophy at Bentley College. She did her undergraduate work at Bowdoin College and is currently completing doctoral work in philosophy and religious studies at Harvard University.

Hoffman and Moore are coeditors of a special edition of the *Journal of Business Ethics* which is devoted to presentations given at the Center's first three National Conferences on Business Ethics. They are coauthors of the article "What is Business Ethics? A Reply to Peter Drucker." In addition, they are coauthoring an anthology on business ethics, to be published by McGraw-Hill.

DATE DUE

MA

E

I

H